# Unwill

# Emigrants

*letters of a convict's wife*

*if there is ever a chance
of our being permitted to join
you again even though it be
in a far off land, both the
children and myself will most
gladly do so ... I cannot
give you up. I live in the hope of
our being together again somewhere
before we end our days — My best
love to you, the children also send
their love to you, and love and
remembrance from all friends
your affectionate wife — Myra Sykes*

Born in 1908 in Perth, Western Australia, Alexandra Hasluck was a fifth generation Australian and a graduate of The University of Western Australia. A social historian and a full-time writer, she was created a Dame of the Order of Australia for her services to Australian letters. She published thirteen books, including *Portrait with Background* (1955), *Audrey Tennyson's Vice-Regal Days* (1978) and *Portrait In a Mirror* (1981). *Portrait With Background* was reissued as *Georgiana Molloy: Portrait With Background* by Fremantle Arts Centre Press in 2002.

A L E X A N D R A   H A S L U C K

# Unwilling
# Emigrants

*letters of a convict's wife*

**FREMANTLE ARTS CENTRE PRESS**

*Australia's finest small publisher*

Published 1991 by
FREMANTLE ARTS CENTRE PRESS
25 Quarry Street, Fremantle
(PO Box 158, North Fremantle 6159)
Western Australia.
www.facp.iinet.net.au

Reissued 2002.

First published 1959 by
Oxford University Press, Melbourne, Australia.

Production Vanessa Rycroft.
Cover Design Marion Duke.
Typeset by Fremantle Arts Centre Press.
Printed by Success Print.

National Library of Australia
Cataloguing-in-publication data

   Hasluck, Alexandra, 1908–1993.
   Unwilling emigrants.

   Bibliography.
   Includes index.

   ISBN 1 86368 395 X.

   1. Sykes, William, 1827–1891. 2. Prisoners — Western
   Australia — Biography. 3. Penal colonies — Western
   Australia. 4. Western Australia — Exiles. I. Title

994.1

The State of Western Australia has made an investment
in this project through ArtsWA in association with the
Lotteries Commission.

# Contents

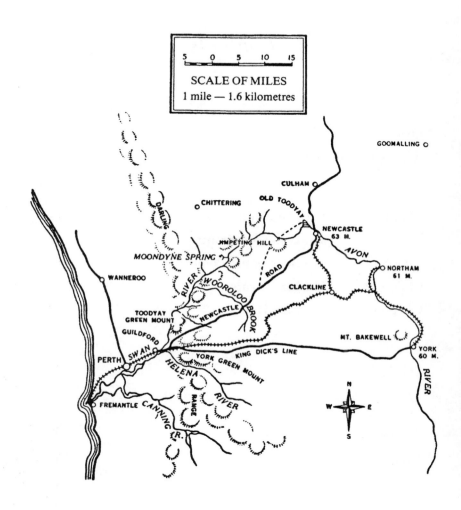

The eastern districts 'over the hills'

*(Reproduced by courtesy of the Surveyor-General of Western Australia.)*

# *Prologue*

AN author is sometimes asked: 'What made you write your book?' and it is not always easy to call to mind the inspiration. In the case of the present work, however, a compelling curiosity, aroused by a set of interesting circumstances, was the starting point.

In the year 1931, a small bundle of tattered letters was handed in to the Western Australian Historical Society at one of its Council meetings by a member, Mr John Stoddart. The letters were in a grey kangaroo-skin pouch, fur side out, envelope-shaped and a bit torn. The bundle had been found in a crevice during the pulling down of old police buildings at Toodyay — a country town sixty-three miles north-east of Perth — and had been handed to Mr Stoddart by a friend, who thought he might be interested in it.

The members of the Historical Society Council examined the letters briefly, and the Research Secretary and Keeper of the Records said that she thought they ought to be destroyed, as they were obviously personal letters and of no historical value. This she stated in a very emphatic manner. The honorary secretary, Mr Paul Hasluck — a young man intensely interested in the history of his State — thought otherwise, and said so. The Council meeting decided that he should take the letters, examine them more thoroughly, and report to the next meeting. Fearing that the Council might then decide that the letters should be destroyed, he copied them exactly, kept the copies, and handed the originals back to the Research Secretary. He reported to the next meeting of the Council that the letters appeared to be written to a convict by his wife, and recommended that they be retained. The Council then decided that they should be kept for the time being.

A week or two after the first meeting Mr Hasluck went to Toodyay hoping to find out something about the bundle of letters. He saw and noted the position of the building being demolished. Papers were scattered everywhere blowing in the wind, most of them blank official forms. One of the workmen told him that a great many papers had been taken by passers-by.

In 1934 the question of the Toodyay letters came before the Historical Society again. The honorary secretary, Mr Hasluck, had leave of absence from May to November, and for that period the acting secretary was his wife, the present writer. The Minutes of the Council for 24 October 1934 state:

> The Research Secretary drew attention to the fact that a series of letters written to a convict were among the records of the Society. She asked whether they should be handed to the State Archives Board to be placed among its closed records. After some discussion, it was decided that only official papers should be handed over, the letters being retained by the Society.

Apart from this secretarial phrasing, the writer has a vivid recollection of the discussion that took place that evening in

1934 on the matter of the Toodyay letters. The small room, carpeted with several strips of crimson carpeting, was lit by the harsh light of a bare electric bulb. Almost every inch of the walls was hung with old photographs. Everyone sat uncomfortably on hard chairs and benches, growing more uncomfortable as feelings rose. For the Research Secretary began by demanding, as she had done before, that the Toodyay letters be destroyed. In a high and somewhat excited voice, she said that she thought as these were letters of an extremely personal nature that no one else was supposed to read except the convict to whom they were written, they should be burnt. The writer, who had read the letters, and some of the members of the Council, were genuinely shocked that anyone should think of destroying historical records. The Research Secretary, growing more agitated, retorted that they were *not* historical records: they contained no reference to historical events, places or personages; they described only the feelings of the convict's wife, and were extremely pathetic. They should not be seen by every Tom, Dick and Harry.

Argument raged fiercely, and quite often irrelevantly. No one discussed what constitutes an historical record. Some members, who had not read the letters and relied on the Research Secretary's assertion that they were very pathetic and had absolutely no historical value, were inclined to think that they should be burnt, their reason being that the convict period of Western Australia's history was one best forgotten. They spoke very feelingly on this. The writer, then a rather shy and reserved girl, was moved to reply that whether that period were best forgotten or not, the convicts had had their part in the making of the State; they could not be disregarded,

9

for during that time progress was made that was badly needed: the roads, the public buildings, who made those but the convicts? The discussion veered off on to what buildings had or had not been built by convict labour. Brought back to the point by the chairman, the meeting was again addressed by the Research Secretary in a fiery speech about the rights of individuals to keep their private letters private. If their feelings were deep, and sprang from the hidden depths of the heart, what right had the Historical Society to make them public? Someone remarked that the writers of such letters were now dead and that their pain and heart-break were part of the history of Australia and should not be pushed aside and forgotten. A member of one of the Old Families of Western Australia said that the State had been founded as a free colony by gentlefolk: the convicts came later and unwanted, and should not be associated with it. But no one would associate them with the founding, only with the making, said someone else. That was immaterial: they were not there at the beginning, they did not take any of the risks, replied the Old Family firmly. But they gave the work of their hands and often their lives, said another member. There were not many convicts; does it matter if one is forgotten, asked another. The chairman rapped the table again, and the writer quelled her diffidence sufficiently to say, if these letters *were* personal letters to a convict, nevertheless they were letters that he had apparently valued and had kept carefully in a pouch made specially to preserve them. Such a thing was a trust to the people who found it. And as the letters were handed on to the Society the Council had no right to destroy them. It was the Council's duty to take them into safe keeping.

After this, as the Minutes say, it was decided that the letters should still be retained. The Research Secretary interpreted literally the decision of the meeting that they should be in safe keeping, and kept them so safe that nothing more was heard of them, no research done on them.

Some twenty-odd years later, the writer, turning over some papers at home, came upon the copies of the Toodyay letters made by Mr Hasluck in 1931, and was again moved by the pathos of the love expressed in them. In spite of their illiteracy, these letters had sometimes a quality of pure poetry; what was felt by that loving heart whose expressions they were had had to be got down on paper, even if it had not the skill, and knew few words and no fine phrases.

Recollection of that Council meeting so long ago sprang full-fledged, and with it a host of queries. What had happened to the letters since they escaped destruction? Where were the originals now? Why had there been such animosity directed at anything to do with convict days? What was known about Western Australia's convict period? Who was this Myra Sykes that ninety years ago had written these letters to her husband William? How did the letters get to the place where they were found?

Clutching the rumpled and slightly faded copies, the writer arrived at the final query — why not find out?

Inquiries at the Archives Department of the State Library of Western Australia proved that the Toodyay letters were still in existence. The kangaroo-skin pouch was gone — perhaps a prey to moths — and, on comparing the originals with the copies, two of the tattered envelopes had vanished, while an

11

additional letter obviously belonging to the others had been added. It appeared that the letters had been passed over to the Archives some years before by the Research Secretary of the Historical Society.

The letters are for the most part written on small sheets of notepaper, about four inches by eight, with a little impress of a flower spray or some other device in a circle or an oval in the top left-hand corner. Each page contains about twelve lines. The interesting thing about them is that they are written in four different handwritings.

It is difficult in these days of general education to imagine a time when the actual manual use of the pen was hard and laborious. Yet that is one of the messages these letters convey. Myra Sykes had grown up at a time when schooling was not readily available to the working classes. Elementary education was in the hands of religious societies such as the National Society for Promoting the Education of the Poor in the Principles of the Established Church, and the British and Foreign School Society. The children of the poor could attend Sunday school and be taught to read the Bible, but very few of them attended day school, and if they did, the standard of education there was abysmally low. In any case, it was a lucky child who stayed at school till the age of eleven or thereabouts before going to work. For Myra Sykes, to take a pen in hand and make marks upon paper, let alone try to convey her thoughts through the mysteries of spelling, was an ordeal made worse by the realization of her own awkwardness. When she could, therefore, she must have got other people to write for her, until her youngest son, William, whose schooling was an improvement on hers, could take on the task. Yet through all the letters can be heard Myra's own voice; the style of expression is hers. Other hands may have held the pen; they only copied what the soft voice said in its broad Yorkshire accent — in accurate English if they could spell, phonetically, if they could not. The lack of punctuation and the bad spelling make the letters not easy, and in places sometimes quite impossible, to comprehend.

Intrinsically, the letters are not interesting. Little beyond family information is conveyed in them, although after research had revealed William Sykes's story, some of the references became clear. If William Sykes's replies to them had been available, their interest might have been greater; but, as will be seen, Sykes was a very bad correspondent. The chief value of the letters is that they arouse interest in two people and a period. What sort of woman was Myra Sykes, poor and illiterate, yet whose words sometimes tear at the heart-strings, and what sort of a convict did she write them to? What sort of man was it that could inspire such faithful love? What was his crime, and what became of him?

Some of the answers were there to find, buried in old Census records and church registers, prison registers, office files and newspapers. The more personal ones were not. A correspondence in which only the letters of one of the parties are available leaves many gaps, which can sometimes be filled by plain deduction from known facts, but which often must be filled by the imagination. This is not to the historian's taste. While it is possible to get some idea of Myra, the relationship between her husband and herself remains a mystery. Why did he keep her letters as something precious to the end of his days, and yet not write to her, but rather to his brothers and sisters, as she often laments? The question keeps recurring as we read the letters, and only the imagination of the reader can supply him or her with any answer. The imagination of the reader must also create the picture of the dramatis personae, for while we know more or less from records what William Sykes looked like — he was five feet six and three-quarter inches in height, with light brown hair, grey eyes, an oval visage of light complexion, and in appearance healthy — we do not know whether Myra was plain or pretty, dark or fair. Sykes could never have answered her repeated question as to whether he would be allowed to have the 'likenesses' of the family, for surely he would have kept such a photograph. Whatever the reason, there is no 'likeness' of Myra Sykes, stiffly posed by a photographer with a rose in her fingers as was the custom then, her children woodenly grouped about her. She is nothing but a wistful ghost arising from the faded ink and brittle pages of her letters.

But Myra and William Sykes were once two real people, not very different from many others of their class and time. Let William Sykes, therefore, be the prototype of many convicts who came out to the colony of Western Australia — unwilling emigrants every one of them — and we shall see what happened to him, and to them.

# Acknowledgements

IN the course of research both in Australia and in England I received the help of many persons and institutions. In Australia I acknowledge with gratitude the courtesy of the Comptroller General, Prisons Department of Western Australia, and of the Superintendent of Fremantle prison, while I was conducting my inquiries; and that of the Surveyor-General and the staff of the Lands Department. The Premier's Department afforded me access to the relevant volume of the Minutes of the Executive Council of Western Australia; and at the Public Works Department, the Under-Secretary for Works allowed me to examine plans from the Principal Architect's Office, showing police buildings at Toodyay. I wish also to thank the staff of the National Library, Canberra, and Miss M. Lukis and the staff of the Battye Library, Perth. I am indebted to Miss C. Gertzel for the loan of her copy of her thesis, 'The Convict System in Western Australia, 1850–1870', which is unfortunately not in print. I am also indebted to Mr and Mrs R. Spark of Moondyne Springs, for allowing me to visit the springs on their property; to Mr Jackson, the police officer at Toodyay, for taking me round the district to see old identities; and to Mrs Emma Bostock, *née* Phillips, now deceased, for information about early Toodyay.

In England, my thanks are due to the Reverend George Ward, vicar of St Mary's, Greasbrough, for helping me search the church registers; to Mr J. Bebbington, Librarian in charge of the Central Library, Sheffield, and to his Local History assistant, Miss Meredith, for their interest and help; and to Mr Anthony Pullan of Banbury, for information and for watercolours of the convict period painted by his grandfather, Lieutenant, later Colonel, Sir Edmund F. Du Cane.

It is hard to express what I owe to my husband, the Honourable Paul Hasluck, Minister for Territories. I thank him for the use of his library of Australian books, collected with care over a period of many years; for notes he has made and reminiscences he has collected from old Western Australians, and for his encouragement; while I thank our son Nicky for listening with patience and some interest while I talked out the problems that arose in writing, and for helping me visit and search various graveyards, with equal patience.

Dalkeith, W.A.
October, 1958

# Unwilling
# Emigrants
*letters of a convict's wife*

# CHAPTER 1

# Man into Number

To be an emigrant implies a certain choice, a desire to go abroad and settle in another land, to make a new home. Englishmen and Irishmen of Victorian times, who were convicted of various offences and sentenced to transportation, had no choice in the matter but became emigrants whether they wished to or not. Some of these men may have been glad of the change in their way of life; many of them, if left to themselves, would never have considered the question of emigrating, being content enough with the blind alleys of their lives, the ways they were used to, and the familiar places. Having no taste for adventure, the attraction of distant lands was beyond their ken. When the dreariness of poverty forced them into the realms of crime, and they came in conflict with the law of their country, then the convict ships awaited them, the seas spread before them, and the far roads led into the Australian bush. Only the first step was theirs to choose and take, and so often it did not appear to lead the way it did. A night's poaching, such as he had often done before, took a man named William Sykes from a little Yorkshire village to the wilds of Western Australia, whither he would never have gone of his own accord.

William Sykes was born in the year 1827, at Wentworth in the West Riding of Yorkshire.[1] The village of Wentworth was part of the large estate of Earl Fitzwilliam, and was one of the few really feudal villages left in this part of England at the time; for already in 1827 the main town of the area, Sheffield, was a centre of the heavy trades — iron, steel and brass. Factories, forges, chimneys and the clustered houses of the workers of such trades, together with the coal-pits that provided fuel for the forges, were beginning to blot out the lovely woods and moors of a country-side that had once, long ago, been the haunt of Robin Hood.

Sykes was one of a family of six children, three of them girls, and three, boys. Their father, a coachman by trade, died at some time before William's fourteenth year; and their mother, no doubt finding it a struggle to bring up a large family, then returned to her native village, Greasbrough, not far from Wentworth, and there she married again. In the course of the next ten years her family married and formed their own homes, and her second husband died. By 1851, William alone was unmarried, living with his widowed mother at Greasbrough and working as a coal-pit trammer.[2]

Greasbrough was a pretty village crowning a high ridge some two miles from the town of Rotherham, with green fields lying below it. On one side of the main street stood a terrace of small, two-storeyed, grey stone houses; on the other was the school, the church and churchyard, the village square. The Sykeses lived some little distance away, at Far Green, and near them lived a miner's widow, Ann Wilcock, very poor, with a family of seven. Her two elder sons were married, with their own families to keep, and could give her no help. She depended on her third son, Albert, aged thirteen, who was a labourer in the coal-mines, and on a daughter in service, for her subsistence. She kept her other two daughters, who should have been at school, at home to work for her. The only member of the family at school was Herbert, aged seven. Myra Wilcock, the daughter in service, was employed at the Ashcroft Academy, a school for young gentlemen at Wentworth, several miles away. There were twenty-eight boarders, aged from seventeen to eight years old, at the school: young gentlemen from all parts of Yorkshire, and two from North America. An errand boy and two other older female servants were employed there. Myra herself was nineteen.[3]

Perhaps, on visits home on her days off, she met the twenty-four-year-old William Sykes and walked with him along the windy lanes of Greasbrough; or perhaps he saw her at Wentworth, if she could steal away from the Academy while he was visiting his brother John, a prosperous carpenter there.

Youth called to youth, and in 1853 they were married at the parish church of Sheffield, William's brother John Sykes and his sister Emma Pashley being their witnesses. None of the four parties could sign the register save with an X mark.[4]

The first child of their marriage, Ann, was born in 1854. Alfred came next, in 1857, Thirza in 1859, and several years later, the youngest, William. They moved from the fresh clean air of Greasbrough down to Masbrough, a suburb of the town of Rotherham. William secured a good job at the Masbrough Ironworks, in Midland Road, and they found a house just opposite. It was not much — one of a terrace of houses, two steps up off the street, front room and back room, and two upstairs. A dark tunnel led from the street to the back door and yard, serving the next house too. Across the road a stone wall hid some of the ugly buildings of the Ironworks, but could not shut in the sound of its steaming and wheezing, gasping and puffing, that went on day and night. The neighbourhood was poor and unbeautiful, a stone's throw from the new Midland Railway that added one more source of dirt and noise to the surroundings.

Life must have been dreary for William Sykes: a round of getting enough work and money for his growing family, visits to the public house to forgather with his friends, occasional Sunday meetings with his relations. The most he had to be thankful for — if it occurred to him — was that he had a house to himself and his family, when most of his friends and neighbours had to take in a lodger or two in order to make ends meet; and that his house backed not on to a similar row of houses, but on to a brickfield beyond which lay Masbrough Common. Although collieries and coal-pits filled the landscape with ugliness, there were still a few open spaces and sometimes a breath of woodland. Not that Sykes had much chance to enjoy them: he had to get a living in an age when more and more people were pouring into the towns to look for work. They had left the village for the slum, as he had. He and they were lucky if they had work, for there was nothing to do with their leisure. There were no community meeting places except the public houses, and no organized sport. There were, of course, the Mechanics' Institutes which had been in existence since the 1820s.[5] These had been established with the idea of popularizing scientific knowledge that might make the workman better at his job; but when so many workmen could not read or write with any degree of skill at all, they had not many members from the working classes. Nor did the tired worker want to be informed: he wanted relaxation. This he had to find for himself.

In the dull round of everyday life, there was one form of relaxation which had the virtue of providing both sustenance for the clamorous mouths of the young, and excitement to relieve the boredom of the adults. This was night poaching. Even though the West Riding abounded in mines and forges, there were still woods and coveys, and fields of grain within walking distance of town and slum. A rabbit or two in the pot with a ha'porth of vegetables meant a world of difference to the health and happiness of a family. It also meant that the man of the family had the feeling of still being able to provide: it meant he was his own man to go out and match himself with the forces against him: it meant that the day's work could be endured, with the thought of the moonlight walk ahead, the thrill of besting the gamekeepers, the feel of furry bodies limp and heavy, promising a full belly: it meant, though the poachers did not realize it, that Robin Hood was not dead, but stalked the woods again, in fustian and cap, with stick and net and dog, to rob the rich to feed the poor. Night poaching meant a host of things that none of the poachers could have put into words; but if their plans went amiss, it could also mean transportation to the colonies.

Poaching was such a common occurrence that newspapers reported almost every week affrays between gamekeepers and poachers. The tone of such reports is one of indignation and horror, but the common man tended to regard poachers much as he regarded smugglers — as men of spirit and enterprise who pitted themselves against a law too harsh and stringent. The Game Laws had been severe from the earliest times when they were established by King Canute, and they had not lessened in severity as time went on. In the nineteenth century, by an Act of 1828, the first two convictions for poaching brought a person three, and then six, months' imprisonment, but the third carried transportation for seven years; or if the poachers were in a group of three or more, and one was armed, they could all be transported for fourteen years.[6]

William Sykes became a poacher, but whether he was led to it by inclination or necessity cannot be said. He had four children to feed, and though he had a job as a puddler at the Masbrough forge, it may not have been a continuous one.[7] On the other hand, he had been the friend and associate of poachers for several years. He and his friends used to meet at the Black Bull Inn in Masbrough to talk over their plans, and when all was arranged, they would assemble at Sykes's house in Midland Road, and set off in twos and threes to the chosen spot. They were to do this once too often, however, and one particular night was to change the whole course of their lives. Destiny was waiting for William Sykes and his friends, casting them, though they little knew it, as builders of Empire, albeit ones unhonoured and unsung.

It is not hard to reconstruct, from newspaper accounts, the events of the night of 10 October 1865. That afternoon, a Tuesday, a couple of Sykes's friends, named Robert Woodhouse and John Teale, called at his house about two o'clock. Mrs Sykes and the children do not seem to have been in evidence, but perhaps they were told to keep away. Sykes told Woodhouse and Teale that they 'must be up at his house again in pretty good time that night' as they were 'going on a longish journey'. They went off to see two others of their band and tell them to meet at Sykes's house at about six o'clock. These two were called David Booth and Aaron Savage, the latter known to his mates as 'Ginger'. All four spent some time making a rabbit net each. This they did at Booth's home: Savage lodged at the Miners' Arms nearby.

Between six and seven o'clock, six men quietly entered Sykes's house: the four previously mentioned, and two others — Henry Bone, who came from the village of Kimberworth, about a mile away, and John Bentcliffe, who lodged with him. Bone had brought his dog, and both he and Bentcliffe had nets. All carried sticks about three feet long. Unobtrusive as they tried to make their arrival, they were not unobserved. Dusk had fallen, but the light from the gas lamp in the street fell on them, and from the upstairs window of the house next door an old woman saw them go in. Later, she was to say that she often sat at the window with her sewing, and she had often seen the same men enter. William Sykes kept a good deal of company, and it was always the same company. She could hear them walk about, and talk and laugh, and she knew when they went out. On this particular evening they

25

left the house in different parties by the back door, going across the yard in the direction of Clough Road.

Clough Road led past Masbrough Common and out to the open fields. Woodhouse, Bentcliffe and Bone had left first, but Bentcliffe had hurried back to tell the next three, Sykes, Booth and Ginger Savage, that there was a man ahead with the bearing of a policeman and that they had better turn off to another street. They were all to meet at the Carr House Colliery. This they did without mishap, Teale arriving on his own. Then they crossed the railway and made their way through the fields between the railway and the canal. In a lane leading to Rawmarsh they picked up some glass furnace cinders about the size of a man's fist, and stuffed them in their pockets as ammunition in case of a scrap with gamekeepers. They had to cross the canal, and as they approached the first lock-house, and began to climb a fence, Woodhouse cut his hand on the wire and swore. A man came out of the lock-house and saw them, so they quickly scattered and met again in the next field. To be seen might mean identification at some future time. It was light enough to be seen — the moon was rising, occasionally obscured by clouds — a good night for poaching. Some poachers liked a quiet still night, while others preferred it windy, with creaking branches and tossing shadows to conceal their presence on forbidden ground.

When the little band had passed Blacking Mill, they came to some fields that looked a good prospect. They set their long net in one, and with the help of Bone's dog, drove the field towards the net. Only three rabbits resulted from this, so the net was pulled up and they went on to Silver Wood. This

26

was an extensive wood through which a public foot-path ran. There were seed fields adjacent to it, and it was a favourite place of poachers, for game was plentiful there. They were undeterred by the fact that the shooting rights over Silver Wood and adjoining property belonged to a Mr Henry Jubb, who lived in Rotherham. He was a well-to-do retired solicitor who, with some other gentlemen of his acquaintance, liked to preserve game for their sport. Mr Henry Jubb was well-fed, and had no children to look up at him with reproachful eyes, too large in pale faces.

Mr Jubb, however, had the prevailing ideas about the ownership of wild animals, and paid three keepers to watch his game for him. They were John Hawkin, head keeper, Henry Machin and William Lilley. On this night Hawkin had asked a labourer, William Butler, to join them in keeping watch. They went to Silver Wood about eight o'clock and hid themselves behind the hedge that separated the wood from the seed field. Machin had brought his dog, a black retriever. Later, they were all to give evidence about what happened next.

About ten o'clock, it seems, they heard a stick crack. Lilley got up silently and peered through the hedge. Three men were drawing a net, about eighty feet long, across the field. He muttered this information to the others. It would appear that he had suspected all along that this was where the poachers would try their luck, for he had taken the precaution to fill his pockets with a double-barrelled pistol, a knuckle-duster, and a life-preserver known as a 'teazer' or 'flail'.[8]

'Now is our time,' the other three keepers heard Lilley say

over his shoulder as he pushed his way through the hedge. Then they heard one of the poachers shout, 'Heigh up, lads, they're here.'

Before Lilley could pull a weapon from his pocket, a tall powerful man rose up beside him from the cover of the hedge and struck him a fearful blow on the head with a stick, felling him to the ground. Machin and Butler followed Lilley through the hedge and were met with a fusillade of stones. Machin attempted to hit the man who had struck Lilley, but was attacked himself, and fled. Butler was knocked down, but got up and went over to Lilley. He was knocked down again. There was a moment's distraction while Hawkin, who was less agile than the others, got into the field and drew the attention of the poachers, more of whom had now appeared. Shouts and oaths and the noise of blows filled the air. Machin was running hard down the field with several men after him. Hawkin was struck by a stone on the side of the head, which 'sillied' him for a time, as he said afterwards, and he made back for the wood; nevertheless, he and the others had all seen, in the scanty moonlight, three men standing over the prostrate form of Lilley, their sticks rising and falling, 'paying' him, as Butler described it. Butler lay where he was and was dimly conscious of the dull thud of blows on Lilley.

Hawkin then went to get help, and Machin also got away, pursued by the poachers. He had let his dog slip, and it was fighting with the poachers' dog, their snarling mingling with the other hideous noises that broke the still night. Butler managed to creep unnoticed a little distance away and got to his feet. He had not gone far when the three men who had been beating Lilley came after him, knocked him down and beat him while he was on the ground. He cried out to them for mercy and swore he would never bother them again.

'Don't pay me any more, and I'll never come again,' he begged.

A man whom Butler later learned was Sykes had just hit him a heavy blow over the head, when Woodhouse came up from chasing Machin, and caught Sykes by the shoulder.

'For God's sake, don't kill the man! Come away,' he shouted. Sykes flung down his broken stick, and Butler got up and staggered off. Woodhouse then went over to where Lilley still lay, and fetched him a blow on the leg to see if he was 'movable'.

From the moment Lilley had burst into the field, Sykes had panicked. It was he who had shouted, 'Heigh up, they're here.' It would seem from what was said in evidence later that he and Teale knew Lilley, and Lilley knew them. If Lilley could identify them as being there that night it was dangerous for them. The solution was to knock him insensible before he could recognize them in the half-darkness. It was also suggested later that they knew he carried heavy weapons. Though Teale had struck the first blow and brought Lilley down, Sykes had joined him in raining a hail of blows on the unfortunate keeper. He had completely lost his head. The next few moments, caught in a net of Time, were to stay with him ever afterwards, recurring in sleep, in dreams, when he would see again the moonlight-dappled field, and the dark body at his feet, smell the damp earth and the sickening warm blood and feel again the horrifying urge to strike the inanimate thing which he already blamed for what he feared was to come.

All in all the whole encounter had taken about five minutes. The others began to fold up their nets and kick the brawling dogs apart. It was vital to get away before the keepers returned with help. The poachers could only hope they had not been recognized, and splitting up into twos and threes again, they made their way home by a different route from that by which they had come. Woodhouse was the last to leave the field.[9]

Two days later the *Sheffield and Rotherham Independent* reported a 'Desperate Encounter with Poachers near Rotherham', and the murder of a gamekeeper, for Lilley had died of his wounds the day after the affair, without regaining consciousness. The report added that the keepers were doubtful whether they could identify any of the men concerned: they thought about twelve to fifteen men had been involved, and the only description they could give was that 'some of the men were tall and some short, and that amongst them were men dressed in velveteen coats like keepers and others looked like navvies.'

The police, however, had not been idle. At seven o'clock on the morning after the affair they had gone to Woodhouse's lodging, searched it, and taken him along with them to the Court House at Rotherham where the gamekeepers Machin and Butler looked at him. He was a known poacher and it was natural to arrest him first. But Machin and Butler could not identify him, and he, of course, said he was home and in bed on the previous night; so he was released. The next day, the police brought in Henry Bone and John Bentcliffe for questioning, for Bone had had a previous conviction for poaching. A quantity of netting and a gun were found at

Bone's house. Bone made a long statement accounting for his movements up to nine o'clock on the night of the murder, at which time he said he had gone home to bed. He said he had been out of work for six weeks, and added: 'My wife brings nothing in, nor yet my family. I had no wages last week. I live as I can. I never was at Silver Wood in my life.'

Bentcliffe also said he had not worked for many weeks. Both were released pending confirmation of Bone's account of his movements. That day, the inquest on Lilley was held, and adjourned for a fortnight at the request of the police.

All the poachers were now thoroughly alarmed. Although Woodhouse, Bone and Bentcliffe had been released, the police had commenced investigation of the murder under a Detective-Inspector Hockaday, sent over from police headquarters at Wakefield. Once more the gang met at Sykes's house to discuss their position. It could not have been a friendly meeting. If the old woman next door had her ear to the wall, she must have heard angry voices and oaths as they wrangled among themselves, for David Booth, who was the eldest of them, a man of fifty, kept pouring recriminations on Bone, Bentcliffe, Teale and Sykes, for assailing Lilley.

'You hadn't ought to have done so much at him,' Booth kept saying; and over and above the others' arguments he repeated that 'only the ones that did it ought to suffer.' At last Teale and Sykes turned on him and swore that if he said anything to anyone about the murder they would swear it on him. When he protested angrily at that, Sykes with equal anger went over his main argument again — that they were all safe as long as they stuck together and no one betrayed the others, for the keepers apparently had not recognized them, and there was no proof that they had been in the field that night. He was very bitter as he reminded them that if Lilley had had the chance to get out his pistol, one of them might now be lying dead.

The adjourned inquest was resumed on 25 October at the White Swan Inn. In reporting the proceedings the *Sheffield and Rotherham Independent* remarked that the police did not seem to have got much further with their inquiries, although it did them the justice to say: 'This is in a great measure owing to the keepers, who allege that they did not observe any of the poachers sufficiently to afford the means of identification afterwards.' The keepers were indeed very evasive: they were not going to commit themselves publicly until the men whose brutality might be turned towards them next were behind bars.

The Coroner, John Webster Esq., in summing up, said:

> This is a very sad and melancholy case, one which I fear will be repeated month after month, as long as there are game laws in existence. I think it is a pity that any man should lose his life for the sake of game, but, nevertheless, the Game Law is the law of the land … The case is one of a class sadly too common in the country, and the sooner we can get rid of all laws which lead to these quarrels much better it will be.

The lawyer who appeared on behalf of the relatives of the murdered man observed, 'That is a question for the legislature.' But the Coroner was not to be deterred, and replied:

No doubt it is, but I still think we are justified in expressing the opinion that laws which cannot be maintained in their integrity, nor carried out except at the risk of killing either poachers or gamekeepers, cannot be very good laws.

Whoever John Webster Esq. was, he struck his blow for the humanities. It was a sign of a changing public opinion towards a code and a class. Why should the creatures of the wild belong to one class rather than another? Why should one section of people be able to kill for sport, and waste those things which meant life and health for another section of people? In this, as in other criticisms of the complacent nineteenth century, were being sown the seeds of discontent and rebellion. Even *The Sheffield Daily Telegraph*, which was a conservative organ, came forth with a leading article on 28 October denouncing those 'gentlemen' who would not make provision for the wife of their dead employee, who would allow the Widow Lilley to apply to the parish for relief for herself and her seven children. It stated:

A case of more unmitigated evil than this Silver Wood murder we have never met with. The only man who behaved well in the business was the man who suffered, and as for the rest, what can we say of them except that the behaviour has been un-English on all sides — the poachers acting like savages — the keepers, like hares, and the employers like a snob.

Moved by popular scorn, Mr Henry Jubb and the other

gentlemen who shared his shooting rights shortly after this subscribed a sum sufficient for a modest annuity for the bereaved family. They had been sooner and more speedily moved to put up £250 for a reward for information about the affray, even writing to the Home Secretary to ask the Government to offer a reward and 'the promise of a free pardon to any person not being he who struck the fatal blows, who shall come forward and give evidence.'[10] On 27 October, handbills offering £350 reward were posted up and circulated through Rotherham and neighbouring towns.

Everyone was talking about the Silver Wood murder, for 'wilful murder by some persons unknown' was the verdict returned at the inquest.[11] In the succeeding days, the poachers became more and more apprehensive as their friends and workmates reported that they had been questioned by the police about them. They began to vanish from Masbrough, Woodhouse moving to Sheffield, Bone to Wakefield, Savage to Nottingham, and Bentcliffe to Rawmarsh. Sykes remained at home. He was there when in the small hours of 31 October, three weeks after the fatal night, he was awakened by a peremptory knocking at the door, and descended to be faced by a police sergeant with a warrant for his arrest.

Sykes realized it was hopeless. 'It's a bad job' was all he said, and watched the sergeant search the house, waking the children from their sleep, and poking into dark corners and cupboards with the dim aid of a lamp. Bit by bit damning evidence was laid on the kitchen table: two large field nets, twenty-two purse nets, two gate nets, twenty-two net pegs, a quantity of snare wire and a ferret; but no weapon — no gun nor stick. Perhaps he still had some hope, as he said goodbye to his family, before the sergeant took him away.[12]

What did his wife feel about all this, about the years of continuous poaching that had culminated in a man's death, and the arrest of her husband for his murder? What did Myra Sykes think, standing at the door of her bare little house watching him led away down the mean street, her children round her, awed and silent? Ann, the eldest, was weeping, for she adored her father. She was eleven years old, and she and her brother Alfred, the next in age, could understand what was happening. Little Thirza was too young, and did not know why her mother cried and clutched the baby William to her. The baby was flaxen-haired and was the image of his father. 'William has got long white curly hair, and he was not called William for nothing, for he is a little rip [all] right,' Myra was to write to her husband later (Toodyay Letter No. 5). Now she had to face the thing that she must often have dreaded would come to pass. There is no word of reproach in any of her letters, and the tone in which she alludes to another poaching affray which took place in the neighbourhood would seem to indicate that she regarded poaching itself as commonplace. She was probably glad of the food it provided, and accepted the fact that violence was a natural corollary; yet she and the other poachers' wives must have known that one day luck would fail and the law would catch up with them.

At this time Myra Sykes was thirty-three years old, an ignorant but not quite ordinary woman with a staunch and loving heart, who had far more feeling for her husband than he for her. For some reason that never appears, her husband's family did not like her; and, at the time he left England, her

35

husband did not value her much, for he used to write to his brothers and sisters rather than to her, and she was often long periods without word from him.

> I feel greatly
> hurt that you should send your
> letters to you Brothers & Sisters
> before me — for although we are
> separated there is no one I value
> and regard equal to you — and
> I should like you to still have
> the same feeling towards me,
> and if there is ever a chance
> of our being permitted to join
> you again even though it be
> in a far off land, both the
> children and myself will most
> gladly do so ...
>
> (Toodyay Letter No. 2)

The next time that Myra Sykes saw her husband was four days before Christmas, when with five of his mates he stood in the dock at the Leeds Assizes. They were a forlorn crowd of little men — short and thickset, they were all five feet six or under except John Teale, who was fairly tall, a fact that was to help to identify him in the proceedings that followed. They still wore the shabby clothes they had had on the night they went poaching, Aaron Savage being in a short white smock, John Teale in a long, light-coloured fustian coat with big laps, and the others in less conspicuous garments.

36

The imprisonment to which they had been subjected, seemed to have had a great effect on all the prisoners and there was a marked change between their appearance in the dock and that which they presented when before the committing magistrate. They listened with close attention to the proceedings but none of them manifested any emotion.

Such was the description of the reporter for the *Sheffield and Rotherham Independent* on Friday 22 December, the morning after the opening of the trial. But whether they showed it or not, all the prisoners must have been feeling within them a very strong emotion, that of a furious and bitter rage. For Robert Woodhouse, the seventh member of their gang, was not in the dock with them: he had turned informer and betrayed them.

Whether the tempting sum of £350 reward for information was too much for him, or whether, with the police net closing round, the free pardon decided him to place himself outside the dock cannot be said. He was arrested, like Sykes, in the early hours of 31 October at the house in Sheffield where he had believed himself hidden, and immediately made a statement to the police. Nor was he the only one. David Booth after his arrest also made a statement, which confirmed Woodhouse's, and went far towards condemning the others. Now, in the dock, when the others pleaded Not Guilty, Booth whined, 'I am guilty of being there, but not of the murder.'

Woodhouse's evidence, the main evidence for the Prosecution, was heard first; and with word after word as he told his tale, he transferred the guilt from his own shoulders to those of Bone and Bentcliffe, Teale and Sykes. It was Sykes who was the leader, by Woodhouse's account; it was Sykes who had cried the warning, 'Heigh up, lads!' It was Sykes whom he had prevented from setting on to Butler as Sykes and Teale and Bone had set on Lilley. Woodhouse had said to them that he didn't think any man could take all that punishment without feeling it, and Sykes had said that he hoped the —— would die. Woodhouse, however, admitted under examination by the prosecuting Counsel that he himself had been the last man to go up to the fallen gamekeeper and hit him to see if he could still move. He also admitted that at this time the others were leaving the field and he was the only one near Lilley. The Counsel for the Defence picked this point up, and by implication and innuendo, sought to impress upon the Jury that Woodhouse himself was the one who had had the opportunity to strike the last and fatal blow. The point was not lost on the Jury. They, together with most people in the Court, held the informer, or approver, to give him the legal appellation, in scorn and contempt.

The trial lasted for two full days, and on the third day, Saturday morning 23 December, the Judge delivered his summing-up to the Jury. It took him over two and a half hours. At the end of it, a juror asked whether they had any verdict to consider against Woodhouse.

The Judge replied, with some patience, 'No. He is not in the dock at all.'

'I wish he was,' muttered a juror.

Addressing the Judge, the foreman of the Jury said: 'There is some dissatisfaction about it, but I could not persuade them that it was not our duty.'

The Jury took less than an hour to consider their verdict. The *Independent*'s reporter jotted down:

> Amidst a dead stillness the jury took their places and answered to their names. The prisoners were placed at the bar. Teale was visibly agitated, and had to grasp the rail for support. Sykes, who had maintained his coolness throughout, did not appear downcast, but showed great anxiety. Bone was, to all appearance, quite indifferent, and Booth, Savage and Bentcliffe were scarcely less so.

To the astonishment of everyone in Court, the Judge included, the Jury gave a verdict of manslaughter in the case of Sykes, Teale, Bone and Bentcliffe, recommending Bentcliffe to mercy. Booth and Savage were found Not Guilty.

The Judge was annoyed, and castigated the Jury severely for going against his summing-up, which had pointed towards a verdict of murder and in no way to one of manslaughter. The Jury looked mulish, and the foreman turned to them and said angrily: 'There! I told you how it would be!'

The Judge then sentenced Sykes and Teale to penal servitude for life, and Bone and Bentcliffe to penal servitude for twenty years.[13] In the gallery, Bentcliffe's wife shrieked and fainted. Myra Sykes and Mary Ann Bone looked down mutely at the scribbling reporters; they had yet to realize fully what the sentence would mean, but at least they knew their men would not hang.

The verdict of the Jury at the Assizes reflected the sentiments of the Coroner at the inquest; it showed the dislike of the ordinary man for the severity of the Game Laws. The armament of brutal weapons, the pistol, knuckle-duster and 'flail' carried by the dead gamekeeper had not gone unnoticed, showing as much malice aforethought on his part as on the poachers'; while as for Woodhouse, it was obvious that the Jury believed him the real murderer, and if they could not condemn him, then they were not going to hang his associates. The *Independent* in its leading article the following week commended them for their common sense.

After the prisoners were removed, Myra Sykes was able to see her husband for a few minutes. For the next year he would be imprisoned at Wakefield, within reach of Masbrough, and it is possible that she would be able to see him there sometimes; but never again did she see him as a free man, and the terrible impression of the days of the trial remained with her. Years later she was to write to him:

> you mencend about
> Lucking yong I thort you
> did when I saw you at Leeds
> my hart Broke neley wenn I
> felt your hand bing so soft ...
> (Toodyay Letter No. 7)

Was it of him she thought on the journey home to Masbrough, while she surveyed the drear and desolate winter landscape and sky heavy with snow-clouds or did she think of the waiting children and her empty purse? The morrow would be Christmas Day.

40

From this time onwards, William Sykes lost most of his identity as a man. He became number 8740, West Riding Prison, Wakefield; and later, number 9589, Fremantle. For one person only did he remain himself. Children forget, and mothers die. While Myra remained to keep the memories of youth and give them life in words, William Sykes was still a man. In many a village and town at this time there must have been other wives who wept as they held the difficult pen, sending their thoughts to link a distant continent to England. But we have only Myra Sykes's letters to tell us how they felt.

# CHAPTER 2

# The Other Emigrants

THE first nine months of William Sykes's sentence of penal servitude for life were spent in solitary confinement within the grim walls of Wakefield prison. While there, he received at least one letter from his wife, for an envelope addressed William Sykes, number 8740, West Riding Prison, Wakefield, and postmarked Rotherham, Sep 9, 66, was among the bundle of letters when first found, though this envelope has now disappeared. Sykes did not keep the letter. The earliest one he kept is dated 15 March 1867 (Toodyay Letter No. 1) and must have reached him after he had been transferred to Portsmouth prison, where he would have been sent from Wakefield when his period of solitary confinement was over.

Portsmouth prison was one of the three public works prisons, to which prisoners who had done their separate confinement at Wakefield, Leicester, Millbank or Pentonville were drafted to begin their period of penal servitude, which would be continued in the penal colony to which they were transported. At this date, 1867, the era of transportation to penal colonies was drawing to a close. Transportation as a sentence had been dropped in 1853 when an Act of Parliament substituted the sentence of penal servitude for crimes hitherto punishable by transportation. This meant that men with short sentences did their penal servitude in English prisons, but long-term criminals, that is, men with a sentence of from seven years to life, were sent abroad after part of their sentence had been passed in England, the remainder being spent in the colony to which they were sent. And at this period, there was only one penal colony left to which they could go — that of Western Australia.

William Sykes, therefore, would have known his destination. On arriving at Portsmouth he would have been put to work for about six months. Some idea of the life and routine at Portsmouth is given in 'A Letter from a Convict in Western Australia to a Brother in England', published in the *Cornhill Magazine* of January–June 1866. The anonymous writer evidently had not minded 'separate confinement', with its silence and long hours of solitary reflections, although most prisoners dreaded it; he contrasts it favourably with the public works period at Portsmouth where:

> the cells consist of tiers of iron boxes (I can give them no other name), seven feet by four feet, and rather more than six feet high ... As for windows, many of the cells have none, except in the door, and the best have only a darkened pane of glass about twelve inches by four inches, and their corrugated iron sides

are painted a dark dismal drab or iron colour ... From the ringing of the first bell in the morning till you go out to work, all is hurry, noise, dirt, bustle. In a cell in which you can barely turn, and in which you have everything to do in almost perfect darkness, and which is so ill provided with vessels and other means of cleanliness that to get through your cell-cleaning at all is like working a Chinese puzzle, and requires the most adroit management, you have to work rapidly and ceaselessly, (swallowing your cup of cocoa in sweat and dirt) till you go to chapel. Then comes a few minutes rest; then — I shudder while I write it — the grand scramble for the closets. It is impossible to describe this scene — it is too shocking. Chapel and the grand scramble over, you go to work in the dockyard, and you will find it really hard work ... dragging about wood or iron, cleaning the sides of vessels, cleaning out docks, coaling, or expending your unskilled labour, and running hair-breadth escapes of losing a finger, or leg, or arm — for few escape maiming sooner or later ...[1]

Nevertheless, the writer remarks, it is pleasant to be out of doors again, drinking in the fresh air, and he believes that the mass of prisoners are so pleased to be among their fellow men again, with enough to eat and an occasional chew of tobacco, that they do not mind the worst features so much as does a man of refinement.

We are not to know whether William Sykes minded the conditions or not. When he learnt he was shortly to leave

England, he must have written to his wife asking her to come to see him. But it was a long way from Masbrough in Yorkshire to Portsmouth on the south coast of England, a costly journey for a woman who had to work hard and long to get enough money to support herself and her children. Myra did her best to explain this to William in a letter dated 19 March 1867, possibly getting her employer to write it for her, as this letter is written in an educated hand, even, well-formed and punctuated with dashes (Toodyay Letter No. 2). As well as his wife's letter, Sykes received at this time a long and moralizing communication from one Charles Hargreaves.

Charles Hargreaves had started his career as a blacksmith in Wingfield Street, Greasbrough; and it is possible that he was married to Sykes's eldest sister Elizabeth. He evidently had had some education, though not much, to judge by his spelling and lack of punctuation; but he was facile in the use of the pen, his handwriting being strong, firm and black, regular and sloping, and markedly characteristic. It is quite easy to see that he wrote Myra's first letter for her. His own letter is written on a foolscap sheet of cash-book paper, covered closely front and back with voluble sermonizing (Toodyay Letter No. 3).[2] By this time he was living at Park Gate near Rotherham, the general aspect of this neighbourhood showing that he had gone up in the world. That Sykes had considerable respect for him is shown by the fact that he gave the name and address of Hargreaves in the space allotted to 'Next of Kin' in the prison register, instead of his wife's name, as most of the other prisoners did.

It would seem that Myra did not make the journey to

Portsmouth to say farewell to her husband. Her next letter makes no mention of it, but speaks instead of a box of food and small articles which she had got together to send him for use on the voyage (Toodyay Letter No. 4). She begged him to be sure and let her know that he had received the box, but he never did so, even though she repeated the request in a later letter. Yet the things put together with such loving care, and representing a considerable sacrifice to obtain and send, must have been very welcome on board ship. Convicts were allowed to add to the not always very palatable ship's fare. Sykes must have received the box, for among his letters he preserved two identical lists. One Myra had said she was enclosing in her letter: the other presumably was in the box. They are written in the same educated hand as the letter referring to them.

### List of articles enclosed in the box

Three Spice loaves — 2lbs Cheese

One Pork pie — one mince pie

2 lbs sugar — 2 Tea 2 do.

Packet of Spice — quire of paper
4 books — $1/2$ doz pipes
Bottle of Tobacco — Parcel of
    Tobacco
Old favourite Tobacco pouch

Thread needles Buttons &c

Three bottles of ink & pens

2 Fig cakes — Apples oranges and lemons
Bottle of pickles
$1^1/4$ lbs Bacon
Alfred sends his little pocket knife

As well as the box, Myra sent a smaller parcel of clothing, for there are two other lists, almost identical with each other, this time in Myra's own pathetic scrawl. These are on small bits of paper about three inches by four.

| List of Articals | List of Articals |
|---|---|
| flanel shirt  1 Belts  2 flanel compforter  1 anchif  2 | flanel shirt  1 Belts  2 flanel compforter  1 anchifes pocket |
| caps  2   purs 1 comb 1 looking glass 1 | 2 caps  2 purs  1 comb  1 2 Cotton shirts and Lookin glass 1 4 needles and thread 6 anks |

The ship on which William Sykes was to embark was the *Norwood* (785 tons, owners, Messrs J.H. Luscombe, London), master, Frank Bristow.[3] She carried a Surgeon Superintendent, Dr Saunders, Staff Surgeon R.N., and a Religious Instructor, Mr W. Irwin, as well as a crew of thirty-nine. She had taken on board a number of prisoners from Chatham at the Nore on 28 March; she now took on a further complement from Portsmouth on 2 April, and then sailed on to Portland, where a further batch was embarked, making 254 convicts in all. In charge of these was a military pensioner guard of thirty men. There were also four warders for the gaol at Fremantle and their families, and thirty pensioners' wives and eighteen children. These are all listed as carried steerage, together with the convicts.[4] Two cabin passengers brought up the ship's total to some 375 souls. It was not unusual for a convict transport to carry cabin passengers. Nearly every one of the forty-three ships that brought convicts to Western Australia carried some. They were usually, but not always, officers proceeding to posts in the colony.

The convict ships of this later period of transportation were not like those which had conveyed the first convicts to New South Wales and Van Diemen's Land. The unparalleled sufferings of those poor creatures, the dirt, disease, prostitution, mutiny and floggings were no more; although strapped to the foremast of the later ships as a grim warning was a black spar with iron rings, which was the triangle to which unruly prisoners could be bound and flogged, if it were so ordered. No longer were the convicts chained, half-naked and filthy, below decks for the entire voyage, an easy prey for death, having reached the ship from the hulks, already in a state of debility; dysentery, typhus and scurvy no longer attacked them by the scores; the between-decks, those hell-holes into which the guards dared not venture from start to journey's end because their occupants were as savage as animals, had gone, together with the stench that proclaimed a convict ship, the feeble sprinklings of vinegar for hygiene, the occasional but little-understood efforts at ventilation.

Public conscience had begun to be awakened in 1837 by a Select Committee on Transportation demanded by a member of the House of Commons, Sir William Molesworth, which had reported in 1838 that transportation to New South Wales and Van Diemen's Land should be discontinued as soon as practicable, and which had made valuable suggestions for improving the prison system of Great Britain. These suggestions, followed by others, were gradually put into practice, and William Sykes and his like benefited from them. Transportation itself was nearly at an end, and the ships that bore the convicts to the colony of Western Australia were tolerably clean and not unbearable. They were of a good size — from 500 to 800 odd tons.[5] Some were sailing ships, and towards the latter end of the transportation period, some were both sail and steam.

The feature that distinguished the convict ships from ordinary emigrant ships was an iron grating which reached from the upper to the lower deck around the open hatches fore and aft. Some sort of barrier to escape had to be erected here, and iron was a refinement of this later period. The captain of the *Hashemy*, the second convict ship to arrive at Fremantle, wrote to the Colonial Secretary in October 1850 suggesting 'improvements on the present system of fitting up Convict Ships in England'. 'Instead of the Wooden Pillars filled with nails now in use round the Hatchings,' wrote the captain, 'a light iron framework might be substituted which would take less room and admit much more light and air.' He also suggested the use of iron for the framework of the sleeping berths, which could be dismantled on arrival and provide 'a lot of assorted useful iron' for the Convict Department.[6] Both his suggestions were evidently put into effect, much of the iron used in the construction of Fremantle gaol being ships' fittings. The use of iron gratings round the hatches became common practice and did let in more light and air, but the result looked, and was, a great iron cage that barred the sky — a continual reminder to those below of what they were.

The few days before the convicts embarked were enjoyed by them as a brief period of leisure. There were medical examinations to undergo, for no one was permitted to embark unless quite fit. They were issued with a new set of clothes. They attended chapel and heard, if they were listening, a sermon specially adapted for the occasion. They were addressed by the Director of the prison on the benefits of transportation to a colony where there was plenty of employment, where wages were high, and where they could start a new life when their sentence was ended. They were then marched in chains to the waterside, to be conveyed by small boat to the transports anchored out. Once on board, there was a roll-call, prisoners were allotted to different messes and ordered to number their knives and platters accordingly. They were issued with mattresses (with a little pillow firmly tacked to one end) and blankets. They stood and listened to another address, and then at last they were allowed to mix among themselves. Excitement, turmoil and confusion reigned for a while as men found mates from whom they had been separated, and exchanged experiences and news.[7] In this way William Sykes met again his three fellow poachers, who had been at different prisons from himself — Henry Bone and John Teale at Chatham, and John Bentcliffe at Portland.[8]

Accounts of voyages out to the colony differ, according to the outlook of the passenger. The fourteen-year-old son of a pensioner guard on the transport *Pyrenees* in 1851 saw it as a youth well might:

Life on board the *Pyrenees* passed very agreeably. The guards mounted for duty morning and evening, and were it not for the men with arms, no-one would have supposed (as in fact there was not) any danger to apprehend from the number of convicts that swarmed the decks of the ships. The convicts were an orderly, well-behaved body of men, and during fine weather made the evenings pleasant by their songs and good-humoured revelry ...[9]

A Fenian prisoner who arrived in Western Australia in 1868, John Boyle O'Reilly — a man of some literary and poetical talents — gives another version in a work of fiction based on his experiences in the colony. This work was written long after he had escaped, and is extremely inaccurate in many of its assertions and descriptions; the horrors of the convict ship it describes, therefore, may well have been heightened for dramatic effect and for the sake of the story.[10] A more factual account is given in the 'Letter from a Convict in Western Australia to a Brother in England', vouched for by the editor of the *Cornhill Magazine* 1866 as really the production of a convict. It describes the congregation of prisoners arriving on board:

All are jolly; singing breaks out from all sides. This lasts the first day. Next day the singing continues, but in knots just as you hear it in a fair. After a few days a centralization principle prevails, and the singing becomes limited to public performances in the hatchway in the evening. This, alternating with step-dancing, an exhibition which gives great delight, continues for some weeks. Then it partially loses its interest, and dies out, and cards take possession of the ship, maintaining their ascendancy to the close of the voyage. By day there are faint attempts on the part of the scripture-reader to carry on a school, but they come to nothing. The greater part of the day is divided between cleaning the berths and decks, washing and cooking, smoking and reading. There will be a few fights. These begin shortly after the men are put on salt rations, and continue at intervals through the voyage. They are seldom interfered with, it being thought best to let the men settle their quarrels among themselves in their own way. The rations are sound and good — good pork, good pease-soup, good plum dough.[11]

The apparently normal ship's life as shown by this convict had, however, its less admirable side. On deck, lounging and smoking and talking, in the light of day and swept by the clean sea winds, the men were reasonably contented and amenable; but when shut below for the night, herded together in the darkness, no light to be seen but the distant stars caught in the bars over the hatch — that was the time when fear of the night with its dreams, and fear of the future in an unknown land, with England never to be regained, brought forth a spate of talk, boastful, repetitive and horrible, from souls quite uninhibited:

In those hours during which you are shut down below — hours in which no officer dare show his face — the atmosphere is for foul conversation a little hell. You then see human nature, not in its highest form of development, wholly unrestrained in word or thought. What the heart suggests is spoken without shame or hesitation. There is no savageness or brutality — nothing of the kind; but filthiness beyond belief. The god of the professional thief is not Satan but Beelzebub; not the god of hate and pride, but of lewdness and dirt ...[12]

What William Sykes thought of this we do not know, for he was not the sort of man to say, although he kept a diary of the voyage. He was more concerned with setting down the events of this, the first and only sea voyage of his life. Yet in its brief and inarticulate fashion, short as his diary is — only one sheet of paper, with a small impress of a flower spray in an oval in the top left corner, closely written in pencil, faint and very rubbed — it tells the whole story of the voyage. There is a gap of a month in the dates after leaving England, during which time Sykes may well have been too seasick to write, for the ship had encountered heavy gales in the Channel and as far south as the Canaries. In fact, it was not until they had entered the calm of the tropics and were nearly to the Equator that Sykes picked up his pencil, perhaps at the bidding of Mr Irwin, the Religious Instructor, whose task it was to impart a little education to those who were in any degree literate, as well as to conduct reading of the Scriptures and other devotional exercises, and give moral addresses —

such points being selected as may appear most calculated to interest, enlighten and improve the minds of the hearers and ... to correct and enlarge their views of the perfections and character of God.[13]

Of this last, no doubt, they needed to be convinced.

*Diary of William Sykes*
On Board the 2d of April
Sailed from Portland the 18
head wind ruff night
the Sattedy night before
Easter and Easter Settedy
night Caut a Shark on the
21st of May a Death the same
Day a funeral the 22nd
A ship came up and took
Letters the 23 a good Breas of
wind 24 A Birth on the 26th
Crosed the line the same day 26
which was Sunday
the outlandic Ocan the tropic
the medary Island the cannary
Island the peak of tinereff
along the coast of affrecca
and other peak mountains
8 days brees. Steady wind 2 June
good wind 3 making preparation

for ruff wether 4 oppisit Eugener
Brassil out of the tropic 6 fair
wind not much of it
7 niggers friday night
8 strong wind boult in the flihg
jib broke out 9 — 10 good sailing

11 Strong not in faver 14 fare wind
squaly albertrosses ollegok cape pigen
and other Birds 19 wind in faver
but very could dail and rain
very strong sea rowling      dreams
very ruff night 20 dull with strong
swell on 21 Birth died 22 wet
miseruble day with fair wind
23 fare wind going well but squalls
24 and 25 changuble 26 ackedent
with the Boiler and too men
scolded July 1 sailing very fast
with squall until the 9 and
then calm and dull

The *Norwood* did not put into Cape Town. It was the
custom then, after crossing the meridian of Greenwich, to run
down easting into the 'Roaring Forties', and across to
Australia on that latitude. Albatrosses and other birds
swooping and following the ship caught the convicts'
interest, and the sailors told them their names. As they
neared their journey's end the weather grew worse. It was
mid-winter. Sykes ends his diary with the words 'calm and
dull', but this was only the calm before the storm, for as they
approached the coast of Western Australia the wind blew too
heavily for the ship to make landfall and they hove to with
close-reefed topsails. When the gale moderated on the
morning of 13 July 1867, they sailed on and sighted the
lighthouse on Rottnest Island at 2.30 that afternoon. As the
island grew closer, the men clustering the sides of the vessel

could see its rocky shape drenched in clouds of spray from the huge breakers. A pilot boat put out from it and after a rough passage, a Customs officer boarded the ship at 5 p.m. The *Norwood* slowly made her way into Gage's Roads and dropped anchor.

> The conduct of the prisoners on board was generally very good and but few and slight punishments had to be inflicted; only one death (a convict) of debilitated constitution, and four births took place on the voyage. The convicts were promptly landed on the afternoon of Sunday 14th.

So the *Perth Gazette* reported to its readers the following Friday. The landing was achieved by means of barges which came alongside to transport the convicts across the half mile or so of water to a small jetty, on to which they would step in orderly fashion and march in single file to the prison. While they waited on deck for the barges to come out from shore, the men stared across the choppy water at their new country. A long low line of dense bush dark against the grey winter sky, the land looked almost as uninhabited as it must have appeared to the first emigrants arriving nearly forty years before. There was, however, one point conspicuous to these later emigrants which the first settlers would not have seen or ever thought to see — a long white, walled building on a ridge behind the little sprawling town — Fremantle gaol or, as it was usually called, the 'Convict Establishment'.

CHAPTER 3

# The State of the Colony

THE colony of Western Australia had been founded in 1829 as the first colony of free men in Australia. The settlers who had emigrated from the British Isles with high hopes for their fortunes in the new country were men of capital, large or small; many of them were gentlemen by birth who had brought out their families, goods and servants, attracted by the conditions under which the colony was founded. 'It is not intended that any convicts or other description of prisoners be sent to this new settlement,' ran the circular put out by the Colonial Office in 1829 for the information of those who did not care to chance their fortunes or settle their families in the convict colonies of New South Wales and Van Diemen's Land. It might be thought that these settlers were deserving of sympathy therefore, when, after two decades, their free colony was made a penal settlement; and so in a way they were, for circumstances beyond their control brought about the necessity for the change. But the fact remains, that they themselves asked the Government of Great Britain to 'erect this colony into a regular penal settlement'.

This was not a decision lightly made, nor were the settlers in unanimous agreement about it. Many of them considered that they were betraying their children's heritage in agreeing to it; but hard common sense insisted that their children would *have* no heritage if the colony failed, and all their capital were lost.

The first decade of life at Swan River had shown the settlers that the generous grants of land — forty acres for every £3 of capital brought into the colony — to which their capital entitled them were of little use without sufficient labour to work them. From the capitalists' point of view, too many of the men who came out as labourers soon saved enough to acquire land at the minimum price of 5s. an acre which was fixed in 1831, and set themselves to becoming landowners and employers of labour in their own right. This would not have mattered if a constant flow of fresh labour had entered the colony; but when in 1841 the British Government set the sale price of Crown Lands throughout Australia at a fixed rate of £1 per acre, and changed it in 1842 to a minimum rate of £1 per acre, the receipts from sales to be employed as a fund for emigration and public works, the colonists of Swan River felt that they had been deeply wronged. Who was going to emigrate to Western Australia when they had to pay the same price for land there as they would in the more firmly established and more fully developed colonies? The colonists could well imagine that fresh capital was not going to enter the colony and that there would consequently be no fund to encourage emigration of labour; and without labour their venture would fail. They knew very well where to lay the blame for this state of affairs.

Western Australia as a colony was jealous of the more recently formed colony of South Australia, and many settlers at Swan River blamed the Wakefield system of colonization for their condition at this period. It had been a tenet of the Wakefield plan that land should be sold at a price sufficient to prevent the labouring classes from saving enough to buy it until several years had passed, during which time they would remain labourers, and the funds gained from the sale of land would be employed to bring out fresh labourers. Since South Australia had been founded on this theory, the British Government had raised the price of land throughout Australia first to 12s. per acre in 1839 to protect the sales in South Australia, and then in 1841 to £1 per acre. No doubt, taking a long-range view, this did prevent too large tracts of land coming into the hands of too few people but, taking into account the special conditions of Western Australia, where much of the discovered country was poor quality for farming and large areas were needed to support sheep, the price of £1 per acre was undoubtedly hard. The huge extent of the colony could not be envisaged by the British Government, nor the fact that more land was essential to landowners here than in the more fertile regions of Australia. It was, however, very obvious to those who lived in the colony.

In 1845, the Governor of Western Australia was obliged to send forward to the Secretary of State for the Colonies a despatch enclosing a series of resolutions of the Legislative Council of Western Australia on the iniquitous price of land;

and His Excellency felt called on to remark that since the introduction of the £1 price, only £65 had been received by sale of land in the colony.

> The settlers of property in this Colony find themselves in very difficult and straitened circumstances. They are all without exception either Farmers or Flock-holders; and the population receiving no addition to its numbers from a regular and continuous Immigration, is not sufficient to relieve them from the yearly increasing produce which they may have to dispose of, and upon the sale and profits of which their prosperity depend.[1]

No emigrants at all arrived in 1845; and to add insult to injury, a Mr Owen visiting Perth from South Australia, advertised in the newspaper that he would be at his hotel at a certain hour and day for the purpose of answering questions and giving information about South Australia and its prosperous conditions with a view to attracting possible settlers there. He drew quite a large assembly, some of whom at times got restive and out of hand when he referred to Western Australia as 'this sand-hole', and to South Australia as 'the Land of Promise'. *The Inquirer,* reporting the event, cautioned its readers, particularly the labouring class, to beware of being taken in, and enticed to South Australia. Nevertheless, there were 129 departures from the colony in 1845.

In July of this year, 1845, no less than three petitions were got up praying the Secretary of State of the Colonies for the introduction of convicts to Western Australia. It was not the first time that this idea had crossed the minds of the colonists. In 1831, a tiny newspaper, the *Fremantle Observer*, had alluded to the need for convicts in terms which foretold the very situation of the forties with regard to labour.[2] In 1834, a petition signed by sixteen persons at King George's Sound asking to have that settlement declared a convict station appeared in the *Perth Gazette*; and in 1844 the York Agricultural Society stated the need for convicts, but got no encouragement from the Government.

The York Agricultural Society, a body which was to play an important part in guiding the way of the colony, had been formed in August 1840. In its first annual report it alluded to the want of labourers, and returned to the subject year after year. In 1845, at the annual meeting of the Society, it was stated that one of their members, R.H. Bland Esq., while on a recent visit to England, had been offered as many of the prisoners at the Pentonville Penitentiary as he chose to take, selecting them himself, and having the cost of their passage paid by the British Government. During the meeting, Mr W. Burges proposed, and it was seconded and carried, that Mr Bland and Mr Burges draw up a memorial to the Secretary of State for the Colonies, showing the great dearth of labour in the colony, and requesting a supply from the Pentonville Penitentiary as speedily as possible.

Nothing of course moved very speedily in a world where communications were still conducted by sailing ship, and government departments were leisurely. The York Society's memorial was not sent forward to the Colonial Office till the following year. Public opinion was now aroused, however,

61

and letters for and against the introduction of convicts appeared in the two newspapers, *The Inquirer*, and the *Perth Gazette*, throughout 1846 and 1847. Those settlers in favour of the idea pointed out most strongly how the colony would benefit from the formation of a penal settlement on an extensive scale. There would be increased numbers of government officials, more houses called for, greater consumption of food. Builders and mechanics would profit; so would farmers, with a market assured for their produce; there would be more demands for land either by tenants or buyers. Public works would be performed that were now held up for shortage of labour and money. In short, not only the necessary labour but the necessary capital, without which labour alone was not enough, would enter the colony.

In August 1848 a new Governor arrived in the colony — Captain Charles Fitzgerald, R.N. Almost his first duty was to receive an address from property-holders setting forth their languishing condition, and what they considered the cause of it. He lost no time in ascertaining for himself the state of affairs in the colony, and sent off a long despatch of a very woeful nature to the Secretary of State for the Colonies. He mentioned the depressed state of sandalwood sales, which for several years had been the only remittance for tea, sugar and other goods from Singapore; he mentioned the low price of wool — 6d. to 9d. per lb., scarcely paying the wages of the shepherd — the cost of shearing and freight, leaving the farmer without return. Sheep themselves were down to 2s. 6d. a head which formerly were worth £5. He saw ahead only:

Depression, Stagnation and Despair, if to this be

added the numbers of our Population who are quitting by every opportunity for South Australia, as also the amount of Capital withdrawn during the last six months to invest there.[3]

Matters had indeed reached a crisis. On 23 February 1849, a public meeting attended by about two hundred persons was held in Perth, and a set of resolutions was drawn up, which was delivered to the Governor by a deputation from the meeting. The resolutions set out the state of the colony, and ended by demanding the formation of a penal establishment on a large scale (see Appendix A). Such was the importance of the document that the Governor enclosed it with his despatch. Both papers seem to have been attentively read in the Colonial Office. The Governor's despatch is covered with notes by the different Under-Secretaries through whose hands it passed: 'This Despatch gives a very gloomy view of the state of the Settlement';

This is a peculiar and sufficiently melancholy Communication. The Settlers of Western Australia represent that they possess neither capital or labour ... They deprecate, however, receiving only Exiles or Ticket-of-leave men because Labour without Capital can do them no good, and their conclusion therefore is to request that the Colony may be erected into a regular Penal settlement, in the hope of a large consequent Expenditure ...[4]

When the despatch finally reached the Secretary of State

for the Colonies, Earl Grey, he found it fitted in well with his plans. He had received an earlier request from Governor Fitzgerald for 100 Pentonville men for Western Australia, and had had an Order in Council passed declaring the colony a place to which convicts could be sent, in order to receive the ticket-of-leave men, who had to be connected with some kind of establishment. Now, with the colonists' further request, it could become a full convict establishment, the necessary machinery was already set in motion by the Order in Council, so the matter could be proceeded with quickly; and it happened that English and Irish gaols were crowded at the time with Irish prisoners, with whom something had to be done. Some of them could go to Van Diemen's Land — New South Wales had stopped receiving them since 1840 — but this proposal for a new penal settlement pleased him with its ability to solve two problems at once. He noted, also on the Governor's despatch:

> It might assist in meeting the difficulty now experienced in disposing of Irish convicts and at the same time afford the means of relieving Western Australia from its present difficulties if a very limited number of convicts were sent out to be employed there on public works calculated to promote the development of the resources of that country ...[5]

A letter to this effect, dated 30 July 1849, was sent, together with Fitzgerald's despatch, to Sir George Grey, the Home Secretary, whose department administered prisons. From this date onward, things moved with quite unprecedented speed.

No time was lost in dispatching the first convicts: a fast-sailing Indiaman was chartered to transport them, and even the weather aided them with favourable winds. The voyage only took eighty-eight days, and they outstripped the ship bearing the despatch that was to announce their approach. Less than twelve months had passed from Earl Grey's first accepting the idea of a penal settlement to the arrival of the first convicts at Fremantle: an uncommonly short time for government action.

So it came to pass that on 1 June 1850, the *Scindian*, with seventy-five convicts on board, fifty pensioner guards with their wives and families, and a small staff of officials headed by the Comptroller General, reached the shores of Western Australia — twenty-one years to the day since the first settlers had landed as free men.

The *Scindian* lay at anchor in Gage's Roads for over two months. The anchorage was not a good one; it was unprotected from the winter gales that blew up from the south-west. Soon after the ship's arrival, a squall had struck it and had thrown it up on its beam and, had its port-holes not been closed, it would have foundered.[6] This must have been very uncomfortable for the seventy-five convicts who were still on board. Each day as they swung at anchor on the heaving waves they must have gazed longingly at the shore; they could not be disembarked as yet for a very good reason — there was nowhere to put them.

Straight ahead of them beside the mouth of the Swan River they could see a high promontory of land on which there was a signal mast, and a squat, solid-looking round tower. This tower, known as the Round House, had been built in the first days of the colony as a gaol; it was a twelve-sided building, containing eight cells and a gaoler's residence, all opening on to a central courtyard. A stone wall surrounded the rocky heights on which it stood, and three flights of stone steps led up to it from the High Street of the town of Fremantle. Between the branches of its first flight of steps a tunnel yawned, leading from the High Street through the rock on which the Round House stood, to the bay where the Fremantle Whaling Company had its jetty, its stout whale-boats, blubber house and tryworks, oil tanks and offices. With the *Scindian* arrived, unheralded and unprepared for, this little Round House with its eight cells was all that Fremantle had in the way of a gaol.

Captain E.Y.W. Henderson, R.E., the Comptroller General in charge of the convicts, did not waste time in being dismayed, or in wondering why his superiors could not have arranged the sending of their despatches better so that some preparation might have been made for the convicts' reception. He set out to find the largest available building in Fremantle that could be adapted to housing his prisoners, and considered himself lucky to obtain premises from Captain Scott, the Harbour-Master, consisting of one large wool shed, one stone store, two large wooden stores, one dwelling house and two cottages, with stables and gardens.[7] The site had the beach in front and swamp land behind it. The large wool shed was only partly roofed and had no floor; and the other buildings required much repair. There was no fence or wall around them: a less likely place for the safe keeping of convicts could hardly be imagined. The convicts, therefore, had to stay on board until the buildings were ready for them.

Captain Henderson landed a working party of the pensioner guard which had come out in charge of the convicts, and they prepared a place to hold about twenty-five prisoners, who then continued working on the buildings. They were watched with great interest by little groups of the townspeople, who observed that some of the convicts had two stripes round their jacket sleeves with the letters V.G., signifying Very Good, while others had only one stripe and the letter G.[8] They were a fine, healthy-looking lot of men and worked steadily and well. By the end of June they had the place sufficiently prepared to accommodate the complement of seventy-five, and they were then all disembarked. They slept in hammocks slung from the roof in two tiers, with eighteen inches between each hammock and three feet between tiers; and since the stone store would only hold 150 at most in this way, and more convicts were already on the high seas, Captain Henderson had first one additional wing, and then another added on.[9] The new rooms were 150 feet by 26 feet, and were twelve feet in height. With two tiers of hammocks they would hold 360 men. Sleeping thus, the convicts were no worse off than the soldiers in the barracks at Perth; but at night they must have strongly resembled a nest of maggots twisting and wriggling. The only ventilation was through a tall, round-headed window barred with inch-wide iron at the end of each wing, plus as much air as could enter under the eaves where the shingled roof met the limestone walls. Outside could be heard the shallow waves lapping on the beach.

Because conditions such as these had been more or less foreseen, the convicts of the *Scindian* were all men of good conduct, too near their tickets of leave to want to escape. Captain Henderson had occasion to point this out to the colonists soon after his arrival. Gratified that the British Government had so promptly acceded to their request for convicts, the settlers of different districts, during the month of June, drew up memorials to thank Earl Grey. The memorial of the York, Northam and Toodyay settlers was pronounced by *The Inquirer* to be:

> respectful without humility; dignified without inflation ... Unlike the resolutions of another district, its language is not stilted or overblown — it is simply plain English as spoken and written by gentlemen. It keeps to the subject, viz. thanks to Earl Grey, and a petition for a continued stream of convicts, accompanied by free labour. Its heading: The Memorial of the undersigned Landowners, Stockholders, and Landholders. Simple, yet how comprehensive. These three designations constitute the real aristocracy of a rural district. Contrast it with the bombastic prefix to the resolutions carried elsewhere: The Magistrates, Gentry, etc. And yet there are magistrates and gentry in profusion in the Eastern districts: but they are magistrates without arrogance and gentlemen without presumption.[10]

The district to whose memorial *The Inquirer* took exception was Bunbury, which also thanked Earl Grey.

The Perth meeting to draw up a like memorial was called for 10 July 1850. Before this meeting was held, however,

Captain Henderson felt obliged to write a letter to the Colonial Secretary in consequence of the great misconception which he found amongst the settlers regarding the views of the British Government, and the character of the men whom it intended to send to the colony. He pointed out that the convicts were selected for their good conduct and because they were near their tickets of leave. Some of them would be at liberty to seek employment in the ensuing six months. The Government believed that a supply of cheap and abundant labour was wanted: Captain Henderson thought that the scattered population of some 5,000 souls in the colony would be able to absorb 500 men during the next three or four years. He ended:

> The transportation to the colony of men who should have to serve many years on the public works would bring here men of the worst character and would inflict on the colony the worst of the evils of which so much has been said in the other Australian colonies. It would besides involve the Home Government in an enormous expense which I should imagine they are by no means prepared to incur.[11]

This led *The Inquirer* to uncork its vials of wrath. 'What does the colony gain by this boon?' it demanded.

> The public works upon which it laid so much stress will be but few, and will cause perhaps the expenditure of a few thousand pounds in the erection of suitable barracks at Fremantle — a building which

will be next to useless to the colony when the establishment is removed, as it is more than probable that it will be, should the absorbing qualities of the colony not be equal to the reception of the occasional drafts of holders of tickets-of-leave.

These had also been the sentiments of the public meeting which, while sending its respectful thanks to Earl Grey, called for 'an increased and a permanent establishment'.[12] The colonists were not nearly so concerned with the character of the convicts as with the numbers of them (see Appendix B).

Captain Henderson lost no time in beginning the erection of the permanent prison. He had at once decided that Fremantle was the place for the Convict Establishment for several reasons. One was that for economy's sake such a large building must be near the source of the materials to build it, and there were large areas of limestone round Fremantle suitable for quarrying; another reason was that Henderson considered the improvement of the harbour and the means of affording safe and convenient anchorage was the most important work on which to employ the prisoners.[13] The second lot of convicts to arrive — ninety-eight of them by the *Hashemy* — were set to work at the end of October 1850 clearing the ground, marking the lines and making other preparations for the permanent prison on a rise of ground behind the town. The trouble was that there were not many skilled workmen among the convicts, and free labour could not provide many either, so Captain Henderson was obliged to write to South Australia for ten masons and six carpenters.

It was with mixed feelings that the inhabitants of

Fremantle saw the huge walls of the gaol rising out of the hilly ridge behind the town. The place had suddenly become a hive of activity. Little gangs of men were busily engaged in quarrying limestone on the site; others were dressing and laying out the stones; others again were clearing away the rubble into trucks that ran down a wooden tramway and dumped their contents first along Henderson Street at the foot of the hill, and then into neighbouring streets. These had previously been mere tracks in deep sand; now they had a good stone foundation and soon were properly made roads. Low-lying swamps were drained. Barracks for water police went up near the beach on South Bay, and also a wing of the Commissariat Store, a stone building of Georgian design, of fine size and proportions, its first storey resting on a pillared vault, and having a large central doorway with a handsome semi-circular fanlight. A jetty at the north end of Cliff Street jutting out on to the mouth of the Swan River was built as a landing place for the river steamer, and for cargo and passage boats; while at the other end of Cliff Street, a jetty on to South Bay for ocean-going ships was begun in 1854, and work continued on it at intervals, held up sometimes by lack of funds and sometimes by weather, for the situation was exposed to winter storms. It did not reach its full length of 450 feet till 1859.[14]

Premises for town police, and barracks for sappers and miners, the rows of cottages for pensioner guards and their families, and terraces of houses for the warders began to line the streets near the gaol. Even while they saw the gaol grow, the people of Fremantle saw the town rise around it, to such an extent that Perth became envious, and *The Inquirer* reported a rumour was going round that the seat of government was to be removed to Fremantle. The newspaper denied the rumour, but grumbled that Perth needed well-paved streets, a secure gaol, a commodious hospital, enlarged public offices, and a more suitable and elegant residence for the Governor.

It was just as well that Captain Henderson pressed ahead with the permanent gaol, for although he had requested that not too many convicts be sent out at first, 805 arrived in 1851, 489 in 1852, and in the following year, 1,106.[15] In this year, 1853, there was a scare that transportation was to cease, and memorials conveying the 'alarm and despair' of the colonists, and asking that the colony continue to be a penal settlement were sent off to the Colonial Office. Transportation did, in fact, cease for the other colonies of Australia, only Tasmania and Norfolk Island still receiving convicts. As penal servitude was substituted as the established sentence, the resources of English prisons were enlarged and a demand for the employment of convicts on public works at home sprang up. It became difficult to obtain a supply of men for Western Australia. From this time onwards, the principle of selection for good conduct was no longer strictly adhered to, and men of worse character began to be received in Western Australia.[16] To have come out in the first convict ships, therefore, was a distinction on which a convict might pride himself.

The doubt as to whether transportation would be continued caused a delay in building operations at Fremantle. As the south wing of the new prison was now two storeys high, the Governor asked for instructions as to whether the roof should go on, or whether it should be continued to its full four storeys as planned.[17] He was advised that the work might continue. By the end of December 1854, one half of the building was completed, consisting of 240 cells, 8 water closets, and 6 warders' rooms, with two large rooms 62 feet by 30 feet wide by 18 feet high, wards to contain 200 prisoners in association. The roof was being boarded for slates which had just arrived from England.[18] They were judged to be of inferior quality; and the cell doors, which had also been sent from England, were all half an inch too wide; nevertheless, they were used. The standards of the rails of galleries and stairs were made from the iron of the convict ships' fittings,[19] the convicts who wrought them showing a flair for decorative ironwork, for some of the ventilators over the doors are handsomely scrolled. The Governor was able to report by June 1855 that all the prisoners had been removed from the Old Establishment to the new building. At this stage it looked rather unsightly and out of proportion, a tall rectangle of cells flanked at one end by an associated ward jutting out backwards. It was hidden to some extent by the high outer walls and towered gateway, where the great clock, ordered in 1851, had at last been received and put up over the gate.

Work proceeded apace; the foundations of the north wing, the steward's stores, and the chapel were commenced soon after June 1855, and the offices under the chapel were carried up to the full height before Christmas.[20] There was something of a setback in 1856, when a whirlwind struck the prison and blew down part of the main wall. It fell all in one piece, such was its strength and so great the force of the blow. Chimneys came down, planks whirled through the air, and the low wall of the solitary cells fell too. Up they all went again, only for another difficulty to arise. In July 1856 the Clerk of Works complained that the work on the north wing was at a standstill, and on the chapel too, although up to roof height, for lack of masons. There had been no masons in the latest ship to arrive, he wrote fretfully; obviously he lamented that few skilled workmen took to a life of crime. There were only ten masons among the prisoners at this time, and with only this number it would take three months to get north wing high enough to allow a junction with the roof of the chapel, which was in the centre of the two wings and at right angles to them. He asked for twelve civilian masons to be employed.[21]

The work still did not proceed very fast, and it was not till the end of June 1857 that the roof of the north wing was slated, and its ground floor flagged with Fremantle sandstone, which was found to be quite a good substitute for the Yorkshire flagstone brought from England especially to floor the south wing. The chapel roof was also slated, and the masonry of its gable completed into a classical triangular pediment enclosing a crown, the letters V.R. and the date 1855, perhaps because that was the year when the chapel's foundations were begun, or more probably because it was the year in which part of the prison was first occupied.

Although in some colonists' opinions too much convict labour had been devoted to the erection of the prison, some of which should have been employed on other public works, at least one end desired had been in part attained. The languishing financial position of the colony began to be improved in various ways — not only through the sale of foodstuffs by farmers to the commissariat, tenders for which were constantly being advertised in the local papers — but also through the building trades.

At the end of 1857, Captain Wray, Acting Comptroller General during Henderson's absence in England, wrote to the Colonial Secretary:

> The prison at Fremantle being now all but finished, I have directed Mr Manning to prepare a statement of the total cost with the view of affording for His Excellency's information before I leave the colony, an explanation of the causes of the very large excess of expenditure over the estimate, and of obtaining a supplementary vote to cover the expense of completion.
>
> Very soon after Captain Henderson's arrival here in 1850, he sent to England an estimate for a prison which was returned about the middle of the year 1852, with directions for the preparation of a prison with 500 cells ... Accordingly, towards the end of September 1852, I was called upon to draw out a plan in accordance with these directions, and designed the prison nearly as it has been erected.
>
> This plan and estimates were called for in a great hurry, and with Mr Manning's assistance, I prepared the plans, estimates, specifications and store demands in something under a week, in order that they might be sent off by some vessel then just about to sail.[22]

In excuse for this large excess of expenditure, he said

75

that errors had crept in, enumerating the wastage of timber in the cutting, the quarries constantly deteriorating, and the supply of convict labour being uncertain, all of which added to the cost. Also, the prison was made twelve feet longer all over than was intended, a circumstance caused by the lack of a theodolite, which could not even be borrowed from the Survey Department as it needed them too. The non-arrival of convict mechanics caused wages amounting to £3,292 to have to be paid to free labour. Altogether, the statement of estimated expenditure on the new prison to 31 October 1856 was:[23]

| | | | |
|---|---|---|---|
| Original Estimate | £7,007 | 19s. | $0^3/_4$d. |
| Excess | £7,563 | 9s. | 1d. |
| Total Amount | £14,571 | 8s. | $1^3/_4$d. |

Captain Henderson, however, did not report until December 1859 that all the buildings on the plan were properly finished, and ready to receive up to 1,000 prisoners if necessary.[24] By that time, the cost of the prison was undoubtedly more than £14,571 8s. $1^3/_4$d., and more profits would have crept into the colonists' pockets.

Captain H. Wray, of the 20th Company, Royal Engineers, and his Clerk of Works, Mr James Manning, had been responsible for the planning and building of Fremantle gaol, and other works at Fremantle. They were assisted by a company of sappers and miners to superintend the labour of the convicts, as had been the custom for convict establishments in the Australian colonies since 1838 when Sir George

Gipps had asked for their services in New South Wales in substitution for two companies of the line.[25]

At the end of 1850, Governor Fitzgerald, writing to submit letters from the people of Fremantle which demanded more military protection for that town on the score that the convicts in the Old Establishment, good as their conduct may have been, nevertheless outnumbered the adult population of the town, had stated that he simply could not send more than fourteen soldiers to Fremantle for its protection. As he put it:

> A guard of fourteen men is in truth a small one, and all that can be spared from the 99th Regiment in consequence of the extent, and number of Posts, they now as hitherto occupy all over the Country, and which cannot well be abandoned with reference to the number of American Whalers, who anchor off the different small places along the coast, and whose crew have, and would, set all the authorities and inhabitants but few in number, at defiance, were it not for these small Military detachments.[26]

The Colonial Office replied, informing him that no more regular troops could be sent, and that the pensioner guard sent out in charge of each shipload of convicts should remain on military duty till the arrival of the next ship; however, a company of sappers and miners, consisting of 100 men acquainted with the trades and callings likely to be useful, would be sent. Accordingly, the Royal Engineers under Lieutenant Wray, as he was then, arrived in 1851. Captain

Henderson himself acknowledged their value in writing to the Governor:

> The convict system in this colony is so interwoven with the employment of the officers of Engineers that if they are removed or appointed to other duties, I shall be totally at a loss to carry on the service.

As well as Captain Wray at Fremantle, the Royal Engineers included Lieutenant E.F. Du Cane, who was stationed at Guildford in charge of the works at that station, and also the works at York and Toodyay some fifty-odd miles away; and Lieutenant W. Crossman, stationed at Perth, in charge of the works at Albany, some 300 miles away. It was necessary for the Royal Engineers, in the course of their military work, not only to have a knowledge of road-making and bridge-building, but also a general knowledge of architecture; and it must be said for Captain Wray that the Fremantle gaol is a fine building, a plain but dignified example of classical Georgian style. He was limited by his material, which was the local limestone, soft and porous and subject to weathering. For this reason, he thought it necessary to stucco the entrance wing, and the main entrance buildings, of which the towers at the sides were used as living quarters by the porter and the Deputy Superintendent.

Captain Wray was a gifted young man. In 1854 he had prepared a plan for lighting the gaol with gas extracted from the resin of the native plant *Xanthorrhoea hastilis* (commonly known as blackboy). Governor Fitzgerald had been very impressed with this scheme, and with the substantial savings in the cost of lighting, which Wray estimated would be nearly £1,000 a year. Referring to the 'practical talents and abilities of this most zealous and indefatigable officer', Fitzgerald sent the plan and estimates to the Colonial Office with the request that the necessary apparatus be ordered and sent out. There were various delays, and the apparatus did not arrive in the colony till October 1858, by which time both Captain Wray and Governor Fitzgerald had departed. What to do with the thing became a problem. The Deputy and the Assistant Commissary-General did not think it would prove more economical to use than oil lamps, especially as the prison had 'an immense supply of lamps in store', sufficient to last seven years. On the other hand, Messrs T.H. Carter and Co. of Fremantle stated that some years before they had conducted an experiment under the supervision of Captain Wray with a small gasometer. A 'most beautiful light' was produced, and they thought that gas of the best quality could be produced economically on a larger scale.

The Governor (Mr Kennedy having succeeded Captain Fitzgerald) was faced on the one side with an immense supply of lamps, and on the other with an expensive piece of apparatus. He wondered, too, how the supply of blackboy — a plant requiring centuries for its growth — would last if it were used in greater quantities. Confiding his dilemma to the Secretary of State for the Colonies, he was informed that all the prisons in England, Bermuda and Gibraltar had gas in use, and it was cleaner and better than oil. The Secretary of State thought it would be an interesting experiment on one of the chief vegetable products of the colony, if they were to use the apparatus. He left it to the Governor's own judgment, however. There was no further correspondence about it, and as it does not appear in subsequent Convict Estimates, the Governor must have decided not to proceed with the 'interesting experiment', and no more was heard of the apparatus.[27]

When Captain Charles Fitzgerald was appointed Governor of the colony of Western Australia in 1848, he was informed — so he remarked on a later occasion — that he had the largest government in the world except that of the Emperor of Russia.[28] If, therefore, he arrived with any grandiose ideas, he had a shock in store. Large his territory of government may have been, but its total population was less than 5,000 souls and its capital, Perth, had none of the features of a city, but rather resembled a scattered village of pretty, small, comfortable houses, each set in its own pleasant garden, at varying distances from the street and from each other. Their general style of architecture was late Georgian — two-storeyed, with a long façade of square, small-paned windows, and perhaps a pillared entrance porch. The few shops had timbered fronts, some with bow windows, some with elegant spoked fanlights over their doors. The Church of England had the square lines, long, round-headed windows and lantern tower of the conventional Georgian church, while the Wesleyan chapel had a classical pediment and pilastered façade. Government House itself was in the classical Georgian style, with a columned portico at its entrance, the main building two-storeyed, flanked by wings of a single storey. It faced St George's Terrace; the back, which was a jumble of additions and verandahs, overlooked the Swan

River. It had been built for the first Governor, Captain James Stirling, R.N., in 1834.

The architect for Government House, and indeed for such houses and buildings as were not designed by their owners, was the Civil Engineer of the colony, Henry Willey Reveley. Reveley's history was interesting but one of frustration. Born in London in 1789, he grew up among unusual people, but the Promethean fire that had touched them passed him by. His father, Willey Reveley, was an architect who had edited James Stuart's *Antiquities of Athens*, and had been a friend of Jeremy Bentham, Thomas Holcroft and William Godwin. His mother had dearly loved William Godwin's wife, Mary Wollstonecraft, writer of *A Vindication of the Rights of Women*, and when that brave and vital woman had died at the birth of her daughter, Mrs Reveley had taken the child into her own household for some years. This little girl, with whom Henry Reveley must often have played, was later to become the wife of the poet Shelley, and the author of the ghastly and powerful novel, *Frankenstein*.

When Willey Reveley died, William Godwin proposed marriage to Mrs Reveley, but she chose instead to marry one John Gisborne. They went to Italy to live, taking the young Henry with them. He had a bent for mathematics and natural philosophy and later studied science at the University of Pisa. A request to complete his studies at the University of Paris was refused by the Emperor Napoleon. Several years after Waterloo, Mary Godwin eloped with Shelley to Italy, and there they renewed their acquaintance with Henry Reveley and his mother, Maria Gisborne. Shelley advanced money to Reveley for a steamboat he was constructing, but when the project became too costly and Shelley withdrew his support, there was bad feeling between the two men. Reveley had an affair at this time with Mrs Shelley's half-sister, Claire Clairmont, who was living with the Shelleys, and wished to marry her, but she could not make up her mind to have him. In 1821 occurred what was perhaps the main achievement of his life: he saved Shelley from drowning in the Arno, and in the year that followed, Shelley's great lament for the death of Keats, the elegy 'Adonais', was written. The Fates were not to be balked, however, by Henry Reveley; Shelley died by drowning in 1822. It may have been after that that Reveley went to London to study engineering under John Rennie, the famous engineer and constructor of Waterloo Bridge.

He then decided to try his luck in the colonies and first obtained an appointment as Colonial Civil Engineer at the Cape of Good Hope, beginning his duties on 1 January 1827. The improvement of the harbour in Table Bay was his primary concern, but he did not prove very satisfactory. The Governor called him 'incompetent' and dispensed with his services in May 1828. Reveley was still in Cape Town when Captain James Stirling, with various civil servants and other colonists, arrived on 16 April 1829, in the *Parmelia,* on his way to found the colony of Swan River. Stirling needed a Civil Engineer, and Reveley was easily persuaded to accompany him. Reveley's wife Amelia, a sister of Copley Fielding the artist, went with him. When their days in Western Australia were over, they retired to live in the village of Parkstone, near Poole, Dorsetshire, where Reveley is described as being a landed proprietor and annuitant.[29]

Reveley had also built the Government Offices and the Court House at Perth and the little gaol at Fremantle called the Round House. As well as these, he put up a water mill for grinding flour 'on the Tuscan principle' as he described it, but it was a failure. After a dispute with the Government over a loan advanced him for this mill, he left the colony in 1838, a disappointed man. Though he had longed for fame as an engineer, his only claims to renown are as an architect, for most of the buildings he designed are still standing.

Ten years after he had gone, however, his buildings were all in disrepute, for the fashion of the times was changing. Before the arrival of Governor Fitzgerald, the *Perth Gazette* was complaining that Government House had 'more the appearance of a Lunatic Asylum than of the residence of the Queen's representative'. Not only its appearance caused objection; the place was in a state of dilapidation. The upper floors, which had been constructed of deal, were riddled with white ants. The roof leaked, and though hundreds of pounds had been spent on it, it never remained waterproof. The *Perth Gazette* suggested a drastic remedy:

The state in which Captain Fitzgerald will find both Government House and gardens is most disgraceful. The latter in particular have been most shamefully abused; horses and cattle have for the last 18 months been turned loose in those gardens which Mr Hunt for 6 years spent large sums in laying out and stocking with plants of every kind likely to be either fitted to the climate or useful to the colonists. All these are now utterly destroyed. As for the house, the best that can be done with it is to place a barrel of powder in the cellars and blow the whole up.[30]

Other governors before Captain Fitzgerald, however, had been faced with bad conditions. Mr Hunt had found Government House in 1840 unfinished in some of its interior fittings:

> without an article of furniture, and the colonial funds so low that His Excellency would have been puzzled to find in his Treasury cash for a grid-iron on which to broil his first slice of Kangaroo ...[31]

and he had furnished his own living apartments with his own furniture, which he had taken with him when he left. His successor, Lieutenant-Colonel Clarke, having been warned of this, had apprised the Colonial Office before leaving England that 'the Apartments appropriated for the reception of Company in the Governor's house at Perth, Western Australia, have never been furnished at the Public Expense'. Sir James Stirling had informed him, he continued, that the said reception rooms consisted of an ante-room, sixteen feet by twelve; a dining-room and drawing-room eighteen feet by sixteen and twenty-five feet by eighteen, and a library eighteen feet by sixteen.[32] And they were all empty. He was accordingly authorized to spend the sum of £721 13s. 8d. for furniture, the sum to be repaid from the local revenue of the colony into the Commissariat chest in Western Australia.[33] Government House therefore, although dilapidated without, was tolerably well equipped with new furniture when Captain Fitzgerald arrived. The only thing in that line that he had to requisition was 'a Patent Kitchen Range of moderate size adapted to burn wood, nothing of the kind having ever heretofore been supplied'.[34]

Fitzgerald was apparently privately appalled by the smallness of the place. He had hardly been four months in the colony when he invited Mr Austin, a surveyor, engineer and architect, to prepare plans for a larger reception room. The work was not to cost more than £1,100 or £1,200; but the Superintendent of Public Works estimated the plans as prepared by Mr Austin to cost £2,320. The Governor said he would not send the plans to the Colonial Office for approval unless the estimates were reduced to £1,300; so Mr Austin was put to work on a new plan.[35] By the time all these negotiations had taken place it had become apparent that the colony would be made a penal settlement, and convict labour would be available to reduce the expense. The matter was therefore shelved. It was to remain shelved for ten years. Governor Fitzgerald had to content himself with having new stables built at the rear of Government House, a flagpole erected, and a new wall built, which slightly improved the general appearance.

With a sailor's liking for having everything shipshape, Captain Fitzgerald did not confine himself to the improvement of his own immediate surroundings. On 10 April 1851, the Legislative Council found itself considering a Bill for the Improvement of Towns, which the Governor said should have been introduced in the early days of the colony. He wanted more uniformity: no house to be erected within ten feet of the edge of the street; fewer shrubs and trees around each house because they afforded protection to thieves; no more roofs to be thatched as they were a fire risk, and even labourers could now build their houses with a shingled roof as cheaply as formerly with a thatched one; better building regulations so that houses would not be unstable and insecure a few years after they were put up.

The colonists, sturdy individualists to a man, protested very strongly about this; to fix a minimum distance of ten feet from the street for houses was described as 'absurd and unjust'. The Legislative Council delayed the second reading of the Bill and tried hard to delay the third. The Governor got very excited and barked: 'I cannot consent to such delays. I have plenty of writing to do, despatches — must therefore hurry through the business of the Council ...' and finally got his Bill through.[36] The Clerk of Works was appointed Supervisor of Towns and the Governor kept prodding him to be zealous in ordering people to replace their thatched roofs with shingles. (The Colonial Secretary, on the other hand, reproved him for being too officious in this respect.)

From this time onwards a sense of civic pride became apparent, whether it was shown by public-minded citizens such as Mr George Shenton, who donated a large number of Cape Lilac trees to be planted at intervals along St George's Terrace, so that travellers were to describe it as resembling a boulevard; or by a demand for the Government Garden in Barrack Street to be restored to its primary purpose of being a park for the people. Governor Hutt had taken pains with the garden, encouraging natives to work on it by ordering them plenty to eat and a blue shirt to be given to them at the end of the day's work. 'Those blue shirts got the natives into more trouble than anything else, for they would let the first person have them that would give them a little rum,' remarked a disgruntled police constable.[37] For some years, however, the garden had been rented to an individual who only grew vegetables there. Soon a party of prisoners was employed in clearing it and laying it out according to a plan adopted by the Horticultural Society, and putting in pathways for the convenience of the public.[38]

Perth was fortunate in its Governor at this crucial time. Captain Charles Fitzgerald was aged fifty-seven when he came to Western Australia from Gambia, West Africa, where he had had several years' experience of governing a colony, after thirty-one years spent in the Navy. He is said to have been 'a man of considerable natural ability; shrewd, observant, impulsive and kind-hearted'.[39] It might be surmised that he was chosen as Governor to succeed the sickly Lieutenant-Colonel Clarke, on the score of his good health — which he evidently possessed, for he lived to the age of ninety-six — or because he was brave and hearty, two qualities much to be desired in a man who was going to deal with a lot of depressed and despondent settlers. The position needed a man who would not quail under the responsibility of advising the Colonial Office to proceed to make the colony a penal settlement. Captain Fitzgerald decided that the settlers were justified in their desire for this, and he took the necessary steps. Had the result turned out ill, he would have been vilified for it. As it was, shortly after the arrival of the first convicts, *The Inquirer* was lauding him as:

The best Governor Western Australia ever possessed
— the most popular Governor in any appendage of

the British Crown — the man whose appearance was the signal for discord to cease and despondency to vanish — the man, who by his energy and activity, setting an example to all, infused fresh life and vigour among the dispirited colonists — who came among us in our darkest hour of gloom and depression ... who, with an impoverished exchequer and a poor and well-nigh heart-broken body of settlers to support him, immediately set to work to renovate the all but expiring colony ...[40]

That these sentiments were not quite so evident at the end of his period of governorship was due more to his quarter-deck manner than to his actual deeds. He was extremely active in the community, visiting all the southern settlements and going north to see the newly-discovered galena mine on the Murchison, during which expedition he was severely speared by natives.

Socially, he and his wife Eleanora added to the gaiety of Perth with dinner-parties, balls and routs. One of the colonists records in his diary for 18 September 1850:

In evening large rout at Government House. Seventy people invited. There were about sixty-five there. It was very pleasant, and pretty well arranged — dancing and singing. Young Hamersley was there, and played a good deal on the pianoforte. He plays capital waltzes and quadrilles. Had a very good supper. Were rather crowded in the dancing. Came away after three. Governor very attentive to all the ladies. Beautiful bright night. We danced on the carpet in the drawing-room. It was intended to have turtle soup, but it was too high and nobody could eat it.[41]

As a relaxation on summer evenings it was the custom for the people of Perth to stroll on the road round the river under Mount Eliza, and perhaps partake of fruit in the fruit gardens under the cliff, where little thatched summer-houses were erected in which they could rest from their peregrinations, and eat the luscious melons, peaches and loquats, grapes, figs, bananas and mulberries that grew there. Past the fruit gardens few people lived, except a milkman, who used to trot round to town with two cans hanging from a yoke on his shoulders to deliver his milk each morning and afternoon.[42] Beyond the Mount, the road round the river was fit only for horse travel, not for carriages or carts. A small party of convicts was stationed at this point in July 1851 to begin the improvement of the road; but they were withdrawn in September and little was done on it for a number of years. It was not considered to be of any urgency, as the river itself was so much used for traffic up and down to Fremantle.

Governor Fitzgerald had tried very hard in 1850 to get the Imperial Government to send a steamer to ply between the port and the capital. He pointed out that such a steamer would be of great advantage, in case of an outbreak amongst the convicts at Fremantle, in conveying the news of it swiftly to Perth. The reply to this was that the Admiralty would consent to a small steamer being loaded on to any convict ship for the use of Western Australia, as long as the inhabitants paid for the purchase of it themselves.[43] For two or three years attempts were made to form companies to purchase a steamboat, but at this stage money was still so scarce that they came to nothing. The inhabitants had to do without until 1855 when a Mr W. Hinton Campbell, a citizen of some enterprise, brought from Melbourne a steamer called *Les Trois Amis*, seventy feet in length. Its initial voyage was celebrated by taking the Governor and Mrs Fitzgerald, and various heads of departments and their wives, for a trip to Fremantle one bright April morning, the decks a-flutter with bonnet ribbons and tempestuous crinolines of summer muslins; the only sombre note being the dark frock-coats and cut-aways, and stove-pipe hats of the gentlemen. The fourteen-mile passage took less than two hours. Unfortunately the *Trois Amis* proved too big a boat for the shallows and sand-banks of the river. It was put on to the coastal trade instead, and a smaller boat was purchased. Soon there were three of them — the other two being the *Lady Stirling* and the *Pioneer*. Gaily painted white and red, they plied up and down, two between Perth and Fremantle; the third, a shallow-draught vessel with its paddlewheel at the rear instead of at the sides, so that it could penetrate the upper reaches of the river, brought down cargo from Guildford and its environs.[44]

So life went on its uneventful way, although (unknown to the general public) the Governor and his senior officers suffered a brief period of alarm in June 1854, when Captain Fitzgerald received a letter from the Senior Naval Officer, Australian station, saying that he had been informed by Sir James Stirling, Commander-in-Chief of these Seas, that there were Russian frigates at sea within the limits of Sir James's command, and that he could proceed with a deployable force if necessary. This was the time of the war with Russia in the Crimea. Governor Fitzgerald wrote at once to the Commandant of the small forces in Western Australia, drawing attention to the totally unprotected state of the port of Fremantle, and requesting him to ascertain the best site for a battery. The Governor was of the opinion that not a moment should be lost in making an apparatus for heating red-hot shot.[45] The Russian frigates never appeared, however. Two years later the war was over, Perth celebrating the peace with a holiday on 18 August 1856 and remaining unaware of what it had escaped.

This was the town the convicts saw as they passed through it on their way into the bush. The first five years of the convict regime had very little effect on Perth. During that time prisoners who gained early tickets of leave were drafted off to country centres where quite an amount of building took place, in the shape of hiring depots, and warders' and pensioner guards' quarters; the probation prisoners with several years to serve were kept busy meanwhile building the permanent prison at Fremantle. There were few convict workmen to spare for Perth. Nevertheless, a Colonial Hospital went up in 1853, and in that year a Boys' School in St George's Terrace — a church-like building designed by the Colonial Secretary, William Sanford, whose hobby was architecture — was begun. There was some delay in finishing it, as it was built of limestone, and Perth had not the extent of limestone quarries that Fremantle had. Limestone had to be brought up the river from Rocky Bay on government flats manned by convicts. The school was not finished till 23 September 1854.[46] Another desideratum was then commenced — the Perth gaol, long clamoured for by *The Inquirer*:

> It is now high time that measures be taken to erect such a gaol as will not render the colony ridiculous by its insecurity, or liable to the charge of brutality by its want of space, or absence of proper ventilation.[47]

The only gaol Perth had was no more than a lock-up on the river's edge, small and insecure and unfit to accommodate more than a few men. Native prisoners escaped from it with nonchalant ease. Since it was envisaged that with the advent of more and more convicts, crime in the community would be sure to increase, 'a really good and commodious gaol' was obviously needed. It was begun late in 1854 and finished in June 1856, and was built of limestone, all of which had to come up the river from Fremantle on barges. 'The site for this building is a beautiful one,' remarked *The Inquirer*, 'and it is almost a matter for regret that it was selected for a gaol, as another equally appropriate but less commanding and conspicuous might have been fixed upon.'[48] The site chosen was at that time well on the outskirts of the town. A later generation also decided it was a pity to have put it there, and partly hid it by building a florid Museum and Art Gallery in front of it, dwarfing and concealing an interesting piece of Colonial architecture.

The gaol contained, as well as cells, a chapel and Court

House. The old Court House in Government Gardens, designed by Reveley, which had always been used for all public functions of any character — whether it were an 'Ethiopian Concert' of visiting American singers, or the annual tea-meeting of the Mechanics' Institute — was presumed by *The Inquirer* to be now reserved as a Town Hall. The newspaper disapproved of this; understandably, since the Court House was tiny — some thirty feet in length — and quite unfitted for a Town Hall. There was no need to worry, however, for the Courts were soon held in it again.

The expectation of an increase in crime as the number of convicts in the colony increased had not been fulfilled. By 1858 there were only twenty-five colonial prisoners in the Perth gaol. Governor Kennedy, who had succeeded Captain Fitzgerald and had inherited a considerable public debt from him, cast about for ways to reduce expenditure and came up with a proposal which he put to Captain Henderson, the Comptroller General, that the new Perth gaol should be transferred to the Convict Department for use as a probation depot in which 300 or 400 men required to execute urgently needed public works in Perth might be housed. His Excellency thought the few colonial prisoners, who principally consisted of reconvicted men, could be kept at Fremantle prison, the cost of their rations, supervision and clothing being borne by the local government.

Captain Henderson was not only agreeable to this idea: he accepted it with alacrity. At this stage he had on his hands a number of men with long sentences, of reckless and dangerous character, who could not be employed on country road-making far from secure prisons. They could, however, be used to remedy the lack of public buildings in Perth, about which the colonists were always grumbling, if there were a depot large enough to contain them there. He worked out that the cost of the proposed reception of colonial prisoners of short sentence would be:

| Clothing per man | £1 | 18s. | 0d. |
|---|---|---|---|
| Rations do. | £12 | 12s. | 0d. |
| Supervision | £4 | 0s. | 0d. |

The total expense for each prisoner would be therefore £18 10s. 0d. per annum, or a fraction over one shilling a day.[49]

The newspapers rapidly got to hear of this and were most favourably inclined.

> We hear the arrangement for the transfer of the Perth Gaol from the Government to the authorities of the Convict Establishment has been finally concluded and it will be handed over on the 1st May after which all colonial prisoners under sentence will be taken charge of by the Convict Establishment at the cost to the local Government of 1s. each per diem by which a great saving will be effected to the Colonial Treasury. We understand that for the present the number of probation prisoners to be located in Perth will be 400, to be employed on Public works of every kind in and around the town, the colony being only at the expense of purchased materials. At present convict labour is employed upon the repairs of Government House and the erection of additional Police quarters at the Lock-

up. A considerable number of the Royal Engineers under Lieutenant Sim will also be transferred to Perth and a large addition to the Pensioner Guard. Altogether the new arrangements are most favourable to the metropolis, and will infuse new life into it, not only by the execution of the many necessary Public works required, but also in a mercantile point of view by creating a large additional expenditure.[50]

The Legislative Council — mainly in the person of one of the non-official members, Mr J.W. Hardey — was less easily convinced of the merit of the Governor's idea. Mr Hardey, on inquiring, found that the actual saving to the colony would be £10 per annum. He remarked that a trifling £250, as there were twenty-five prisoners, was not much to save. It appeared to him that the colony was gradually losing all its independence and everything was becoming connected with convicts: there was little inducement for free artisans to remain.[51]

The Governor scathingly observed that the honourable member seemed to consider the independence of the colony lost by removing a few vagabonds from one place to another. What was the use of having convicts, but for the advantage of having unpaid labour on public works? He elaborated this theme for several minutes. Finally a Bill was passed, declaring that:

Part of the building at Fremantle known as the Imperial Convict Establishment shall be ... from the present date a public Gaol of this colony to be used for the same purposes as the Gaol at Perth. Prisoners now detained in the building heretofore known and used as the Public Gaol of Perth to be forthwith removed from the said building to Fremantle Gaol.

It was gazetted on 1 June 1858.

From this time the Perth gaol remained in the use of the Convict Department until 1875, when it again reverted to the Colonial Government.[52] Since 1870 it had been used for local female prisoners, of whom there were few, but who were never admitted to the Fremantle prison even under the arrangement for colonial prisoners. It also held debtors, persons committed for trial, and persons convicted of capital offences.[53] The cell accommodation was inadequate and in 1876, when it reverted to the Colonial Government, it was enlarged. It remained in use for ten years. Then, in 1886, the Convict Establishment at Fremantle, whose inmates were by that time reduced to seventy-five, was transferred from the British to the Colonial Government to become the sole prison of the colony. By 14 April 1888 all prisoners in the colony were removed to Fremantle, and the Perth gaol fell empty. Proposals were then made to alter it to provide quarters for married and single police. Eventually it became part of the Perth Museum for which it was totally unsuited. With the exception of the chapel and courtroom, the rooms are small; and, since its construction did not include a damp-proof layer, the soft porous limestone of its walls conducts moisture even to the upper storeys. It is four storeys high, with a basement originally intended for cells, but while it was in process of building, the Governor requested that the cells below ground level be abandoned as prejudicial to health.[54]

The architect for the Perth gaol was Richard Jewell, the Clerk of Works in the Colonial Government. He had under him a staff of one — a youth to do the secretarial work, for which he had no time himself. He was kept very busy with the hospital and the gaol and other works requiring his attention. He was to be seen riding out on his horse before eight o'clock each morning to inspect the prisoners at work on the different projects, and usually had to admonish them to work better and harder. He had not a high regard for convicts as workmen, as the Letter Book which he kept shows.

Richard Jewell was responsible for the architecture of most of the new buildings which now gradually began to grow up and obscure Reveley's Georgian village. To him must be ascribed the change of taste and the development of the Victorian Gothic style in Perth. He had emigrated to the colony in 1852. A man forty-two years of age, he had been trained as an architect in England and had been employed there on such constructions as the military prison at Gosport, and fortifications at Portsea and Southsea Castle.[55] His opposite number at Fremantle, the Clerk of Works of the Convict Establishment, James Manning, was a contemporary who had had much the same training as himself. Manning had come out in 1850 on Captain Henderson's staff.[56] The two men, sometimes singly, sometimes in conjunction, in the course of the next ten years or so, planned and directed the building of some half-dozen handsome edifices, landmarks of their period, though marked down today in the notebook of the progressive town planner for demolition.[57]

97

With the advent of a large number of probation prisoners to Perth gaol in 1858, an era of building began for Perth. A detachment of Royal Engineers under Lieutenant Sim was transferred to Perth, and Mr Jewell found himself working in conjunction with the Lieutenant. For a while it was not at all clear whether he was to take his instructions from the Colonial Secretary or from the Royal Engineer, a state of affairs which he evidently considered unsatisfactory; but by 1800 he was listed under the Convict Department as Perth Clerk of Works, receiving a temporary allowance of £50 per annum.[58] He was in constant communication with Manning at Fremantle, to whom he would apply when he wanted particular workmen, such as painters or plasterers.

A curious anomaly to be noted about the whole convict period is that although the convicts provided most of the labour for the different public buildings, they never provided all of it. There were never enough skilled workmen among the convicts for the entire performance of different jobs. Free labour had to be called in either to make up numbers, or to fulfil particular contracts. This applied even to the Fremantle Establishment itself, which at several stages had to call in civilian workmen. The colonists began to profit from the letting of contracts for cut timber, or for bricklaying and stonecutting, or for various other building requirements. For instance, in the construction of the new Government House the tender of one W. Harrison to cut stone arches at 6s. 0d. per foot, and quoins at 2s. 3d. was accepted; and the contractor for the brickwork, James Brittain, was told to send a better bricklayer along, or some of the work would be pulled down and the expense charged against sums due to him. It was proposed to call private tenders for timber for joists, for plasterers' work, and for laying slates for the roof.[59] On the whole, the convicts were only fit for the crudest labour, such as bricklaying, slate-cutting or quarrying. Nor were they a stable force to be counted on in planning certain works. There was a constant ebb and flow. Men might attain their tickets of leave and go off, to be dispersed throughout the colony, and whether or not they could be replaced in their particular trades depended on the new shiploads arriving. Changing conditions in England meant that in some years few or no ships arrived, and therefore that there was considerable resultant delay on works in progress.

Soon Mr Jewell had his hands full with the building of the new Government House, the foundation stone of which was laid on 17 March 1859. Though it was blazing hot that day, the largest assemblage which had ever come together in Perth poured into the grounds of Government House to witness the ceremony. Many were visitors from the country, and the steamer from Fremantle increased the throng with nearly a hundred passengers.

The Governor, Mr Kennedy, had invited the Masonic Lodge of St John to perform the ceremony of laying the foundation stone. 'The ancient and honourable craft mustered strong upon this to the most interesting occasion,' reported *The Inquirer,* and described how the Masons walked in procession, between forty and fifty in number, to the grounds of the old Government House in which the new building was to be erected. After a prayer was said, coins and an inscription were deposited in a cavity, the stone was placed in position, the Governor's Lady spread cement with a trowel, the military in their red coats presented arms and the band of the Royal Engineers struck up. The Worshipful Master adjusted the stone with the Plumb Rule, Level and Square, saying at the same time, 'May the Great Architect of the Universe grant a blessing on this foundation stone.'[60]

Mrs Kennedy may have had the pleasure of assisting at the ceremony, but she never had the pleasure of living in the house. It was not finished until 1863. In that year the Pensioners' Barracks, placed in a dominating position at the western end of St George's Terrace, was begun. The need for this building arose because the British Government in 1862 removed all regular troops of the line from Western Australia, and the pensioner guard was all that remained for its protection. The barracks were to provide for the accommodation of fifty married men and twenty single men, and were not finished till 1866. Both the new Government House and the barracks are referred to as being in the Tudor style and, like many other buildings in Western Australia of this time, are built of red and yellow bricks laid in a chequered pattern, in a way that seems to be peculiar to Western Australia.

In December 1866, *The Inquirer* was pleased to announce:

It is, we believe, the intention of the Governor to erect a Town Hall and Market Place in Barrack Square, Perth. The building will be of a substantial and pleasing character; the ground floor intended for market stalls, etc. with, we presume, capacious cellars underneath, and the upper floor a hall for business meetings, public entertainments etc. The entire labour and materials will be provided at the cost of the Government and when finished, the premises will be formally handed over to the City Council.[61]

The foundation stone of the Town Hall was laid on 24 May 1867. It was another of Richard Jewell's buildings. He had submitted two designs to the Governor, one being English Gothic of the fifteenth century, which was rejected; the other, which was accepted, was described by *The Inquirer* of 10 April 1867, as 'in the style of architecture of Scotland of the fifteenth or sixteenth century, more generally known as the Tudor style.' It is plain from the tone of the newspaper's description that, although Perth technically became a city when its bishopric was established in 1856, it could not be regarded as one until it had a Town Hall.

It was well that these buildings had been erected, for the era of transportation and free labour was coming to an end. The eastern colonies had been strongly against the creation of a penal settlement in Western Australia in 1849, at a time when they were in the midst of a campaign to discontinue transportation to Australia as a whole. South Australia and Victoria in particular had protested that they would be flooded with conditional pardon men quitting Western Australia. In 1858, South Australia passed 'an Act to prevent the Introduction into the Province of South Australia of Convicted Felons and other persons sentenced to Transportation', the second clause of which gave great offence to its neighbouring colony, for it stated specifically that no person from Western Australia was to land without a certificate to say he was not, and never had been, a prisoner of the Crown.[62] This 'passport' was required for a number of years, and rankled very much in the minds of the free settlers. *The Inquirer* waxed sarcastic about South Australia's apprehensions:

> Swan River in connection with the convict question has afforded a ready theme for romance to the adjacent colonists. The South Australians have been particularly industrious in painting the gigantic social evil. Not an offence was committed, not a police report appeared, but 'Swan River' was written on it in bold relief ... In their mind's eye they saw at least one of this gentry with S.R. on his forehead prowling at every turning of their streets, and to nurse the spirit of the S.R. they left these streets to watch themselves. With an efficient police force it would be difficult to carry out their performance of the rare old English gentleman, showing the extreme end of a night-cap and the mouth of a blunderbuss from the upper window, on hearing the slightest noise at their doors. They leave their streets to the care of half a dozen policemen, who, for aught we know, have, like those of a different country in a different time, to watch number 1 first, and melodiously indicate the state of the weather at their leisure ... We protest against this imaginary tracing of their criminal offenders to this colony. South Australia must learn from experience, if she wont [sic] otherwise, that a neglect of protection will foster crime into existence. They have no need to look beyond their own doors if they would get crime into their clutch, and really wish to strike at its root.[63]

In the year following this rather tangled piece of fulmination, the *South Australian Chronicle* announced:

> An apology will be due from South Australia to the ruffianry of Swan River who have — for months past — been credited with the murderous outrages of Captain Thunderbolt and Co. These outrages, so unlike anything that could rationally be expected of South Australians, were in consequence ascribed to 'Swan River lags', and a great deal of virtuous indignation was vented against convictism in consequence. It turns out, however, that the Swan Riverites have been maligned, and that the rascality of our own colony is quite equal to the desperate doings that we supposed could only emanate from professional felons.

In quoting this, *The Inquirer* remarked with unction that it was pleased to see that South Australia was coming to its senses, and added that the 'ruffianry' had never been maligned. It was the settlers who had been maligned, and who felt they were unjustly heaped with indignity for doing what they had to save their colony — asking for convicts. 'Our colonists can but wish to see this *Convict Prevention Act* repealed,' it continued, referring to the Act to prevent convicts from entering South Australia and requiring a certificate of freedom from travellers from Western Australia, and ended: 'It is obnoxious to intercourse with a neighbouring colony.'[64]

Perth was now an established city with handsome civic and

private buildings. There were wide open spaces between them, it is true, and the roads and foot-paths left much to be desired. Fremantle, too, looked like a port and a town of consequence. The builders had done their work (perhaps grudgingly and not perfectly) and there was an air of life and progress about the place. The streets and the shops were more crowded with people, even if most of them were men. The sea roads were full of ships. The year 1867 was to see the last two convict ships ever to sail to Australia depart from England, one in April and one in October.[65] That which sailed in April was the *Norwood*, bringing William Sykes to Western Australia. Had his crime been committed only a little later, he would never have left England. When his sentence had expired he might have seen his wife again, or at least his children. As it was, he became an emigrant, and the land that he took up was six good feet of hard, sun-baked Australian earth, his for ever.

# CHAPTER 4

# The Hard Years

·

WHEN William Sykes and his fellow prisoners from the *Norwood* began their march from the jetty to the gaol through the streets of Fremantle that Sunday afternoon of 14 July 1867, they might have been passing through a deserted town for there were few to watch them. No one was going to stand out in the squalls of driving rain off the sea in this wettest month of the year just to see another batch of convicts go by. The people of Fremantle were used to convicts. A generation was nearly grown up who had always seen the grey-clad gangs at work on jetties and bridges, roads and government buildings; who knew that the curfew tolled at ten o'clock each night, and after that the policeman on rounds challenged late wanderers with the words, 'Bond or free?'; who heard at times, in the early morning as they lay in bed, the clink and shuffle of the chain gang going to work in the limestone quarries. The presence of convicts was accepted as an ordinary part of life, and new ones arriving were unremarked. A few children on an occasional verandah might stop their play to stare for a moment at the dingy figures filing by, but the inhabitants as a whole had lost interest in a sight that had been frequent for the best part of seventeen years. Forty-one ships in that time had decanted their convict load and sailed away. The *Norwood* was the forty-second. There was to be one more convict ship early in the next year.

The great main gateway of Fremantle prison juts out from the high surrounding wall in two five-sided towers joined by a classical pediment in which is set a large, black-faced clock with gilt Roman figures. It tells the time no longer. Once its bell could be heard on calm days to a distance of three miles, clanging the passing hours.

This forbidding structure faced the convicts of the *Norwood* with no aspect of welcome as they marched up the slight incline towards it on that rainy July afternoon. The heavy gates swung wide for them, and once inside, they were drawn up for inspection. Then they were drafted off in batches to the ablutions shed, where they must have been pleased to find that there was plenty of hot water.[1] In the summer season they would find that they were taken twice or thrice a week to the sea beach for bathing.[2] This may not have been altogether an unmixed blessing to men who were not accustomed to using much water on their bodies, and many of whom had probably never set foot in the sea in their lives; but in the hot summer, after days in the burning sun swinging sledge-hammer and pickaxe, the aquamarine waters of South Bay must have had some appeal. After the dirt of the slums of England from which many of them had come, Fremantle must have seemed in many respects unbearably clean. The stark white limestone buildings, the blinding white sand that surrounded the town, often caused an eye condition in men unused to the glare.[3] The prison surgeon's reports show that ophthalmia was by far the most prevalent disease among convicts, and no doubt this gave rise to the saying, that Western Australia was 'A Land of Sand, Sin, Sorrow and Sore Eyes'.

Now, after their turn in the ablutions shed, the men of the *Norwood* had their old clothing collected, to be given to the Aboriginal prisoners on Rottnest Island, and were issued with a dark grey fustian jacket, waistcoat and trousers, stamped with the broad arrow; a pair of flannel under-drawers, a flannel shirt and two cotton shirts, socks, handkerchiefs, a leather belt, a pair of boots and a cap. These clothes they would surrender at the end of winter, to be issued with summer jacket, waistcoat and trousers of white duck, shapeless and sloppy but cool, stamped with black arrows, and fastened with small flat metal buttons.[4] Their hair and whiskers were then cut as close as possible and they were detailed off to their cells.

Work was waiting for them. In the course of the next day or two, the Clerk of Works of the Convict Department received a 'Memorandum with reference to the prisoners arrived per *Norwood*':

The mechanics will be placed in the workshops on trial to test their qualifications and as soon as it has been ascertained which of them are fit for work in the

Shops they are to be set to work and a list of them forwarded.

A strong party will be sent to Cantonment Hill to procure stone for the Chain gang.

One pair of sawyers will be sent to Perth. Another pair of sawyers is to be sent to the Collie Bridge. All the brick-makers are to be sent to Perth prison for Claisebrook.

Four volunteers (being men with long periods to serve) are to be sent to Guildford to learn sawing at York Green Mount. None of the men are to be sent as above directed until the taking of their descriptions has been completed.[5]

It was signed: Henry Wakeford, Comptroller General.

Captain Henderson, who had been Comptroller General since the beginning of the convict period, had left the colony on 31 January 1863. He had been a kindly and a just man, moderate and understanding, opposed to the harsher forms of discipline. He thought that flogging as a punishment did more harm than good, and might be utterly abolished except in rare cases, and that putting men in chains was useless and aggravating.[6] The success of the convict system in Western Australia was largely due to his wise administration. He was succeeded by Captain R.F. Newland, who remained less than three years. Differences of opinion between Captain Newland and Governor Hampton caused Newland's departure. The Governor then installed his own son, Mr G.E. Hampton, as Acting Comptroller until the arrival of Henry Wakeford on 15 May 1867.

William Sykes was lucky that the new Comptroller General

had taken charge two months before the men from the *Norwood* entered the prison. The four years since Captain Henderson had left had seen increasingly stringent discipline imposed at the Establishment by the orders of Governor Hampton. This may have been because it was the method he had employed when he had been Comptroller General in Tasmania: it may also have been due to the type of prisoner at the time. In an effort to maintain the supply of prisoners to Western Australia the Home authorities had sent out a number of reckless and dangerous men who were in a constant state of insubordination. Solitary confinement, hard labour in chains, and flogging became the order of the day. Escapes became more frequent from men goaded to desperation by the intolerable harshness of the regime which Hampton forced the magistrates and prison staff to impose on them.

The new Comptroller, Mr Wakeford, while he recognized that men difficult to control needed strict treatment, reduced the size of the chain gangs and the number of floggings, and in his reports stressed the need for efficiency in the prison staff and for a better type of warder. Under his administration, and with the departure of Governor Hampton, the system reverted to what it had been under Henderson.[7]

The taking of particulars from the men of the *Norwood* began at once. The 'List of Convict Ships arrived in the Colony' gives their physical description. Of the four poachers, William Sykes, short, fair and ruddy, has been described earlier. Henry Bone, age thirty-seven, was five feet four and a quarter inches in height, with brown hair, grey eyes, sallow, full-faced and middling stout. John Bentcliffe, age thirty-two, was five feet six and a quarter inches in height, with brown hair, hazel eyes, a long dark face, and was also middling stout; while John Teale, age thirty-seven, was five feet ten and a quarter inches in height, with dark hair, brown eyes, dark skin and an oval face. The prison registers give particulars of each man's crime, sentence, date and place of conviction, and from what prison they had come; their religion, whether they were literate, whether they were married or single, names and ages of their wives and families, and the address of their next of kin.

These last columns are fully filled in for Bone and Bentcliffe. Teale was unmarried. William Sykes, however, could not recall any of his children's ages, only their names; he did not give his wife's name at all: and where the others gave their wives' or parents' addresses for next of kin, William Sykes gave the name and address of Charles Hargreaves, of Park Gate, Rotherham.[8] The impression left is that he was a widower, which was not the case. He may have deliberately allowed the recording clerk to think this; he may not have wanted to mention Myra's name in such surroundings: he can hardly have forgotten it so soon.

As well as their descriptions, the trades of the 253 men from the *Norwood* were noted down. They make a typical list of the sort of workmen who could be expected from the convict emigrants. There were forty-four labourers. There were thirty-three men whose trade was given as 'none', which may have meant that they were gentlemen of leisure, but more probably implied that they were gentlemen of the thieving fraternity: the very sort of convict that one Governor had declared he dreaded more than murderers, because of

110

their distaste for work. There were thirteen miners, twelve tailors, twelve shoemakers, eleven grooms, seven bricklayers, seven carpenters, seven sailors, six painters, six butchers, five fitters and turners, five bakers, five masons, four smiths, four puddlers, four sawyers, three watermen, three colliers, three clerks, three strikers, three farmers, two commercial travellers, two greengrocers, two barmen, two bootclosers, two bookbinders, two car-men, two waggoners, and thirty-eight other single trades, among which were an architect, civil engineer, surveyor, accountant, druggist, practical chemist, engraver, silversmith, shepherd, cooper, hawker, horsebreaker, overlooker, upholsterer, brass finisher, brass founder, glazier, fireman, penknife grinder, blast-minder, cloth-dresser, carter, potter, cutter, tinplate-worker, millhand, gun-maker, comb-maker, boiler-maker, ship-maker, packing-case-maker, gas-holder-maker, watch-maker, rope-maker and fiddle-string-maker.[9]

During the days it took to register their particulars, William Sykes and his mates would have gradually become accustomed to their new prison. The food was ample, if somewhat starchy: breakfast, 10 oz. bread, 1 oz. treacle, 1 pint of tea with sugar; dinner, 14 oz. meat, 12 oz. potatoes; supper, 8 oz. bread, otherwise the same as breakfast. Soup was allowed twice a week, and on soup days cabbages, turnips or pumpkin were used instead of potatoes. The men liked soup because it filled them. The board of medical officers recommended the occasional use of bread made with bran on account of its laxative properties; also that in summer the amount of tea be lessened and lime juice, vinegar and more vegetables be issued.[10] Starchy or not, a diet including 14 oz.

111

of meat per day was more than men like William Sykes had been used to in all their lives. Meat at least was plentiful in this new land, and most of it was fresh meat. In certain seasons when fresh meat was scarce, salt meat was issued, but on the whole the convict emigrants were luckier than the first settlers in this respect, for the latter had often been obliged to subsist for long periods on salt pork or beef.

Recovering their land legs, Sykes and his mates may have tentatively inquired from the old hands at the prison as to the chances of escape. Here they may have been let in to the Establishment's most recent joke. The chance of escape without outside help to another part of Australia were practically *nil*, they would be told: the land was a vast natural gaol, the sea on three sides and twelve hundred miles of trackless and waterless country on the other. The probability of escape from the system itself within Western Australia was slightly greater. It could be done; many had done it, but had been recaptured. The problem was, once having got out, to stay out; and very few had managed this. But Moondyne Joe had done it, the newcomers would be informed and the joke was on the Governor who had brought it on himself.

In surreptitious mutterings, the new arrivals would be told of a cell on the third floor, its walls heavily timbered with jarrah studded with dogspikes, its window double-barred and lined with a steel plate scantily spotted with circular holes. No more than a cage it was, a cage devised by the Governor to hold Moondyne Joe.

When Western Australia had petitioned to become a convict settlement, many people had deplored the fact, and dreaded the days when bushrangers in the form of escaped convicts would terrorize the country, as they had done in the eastern colonies. This, however, had not occurred. Convicts did escape at times, and commit armed robbery, if they could steal a gun from some settler's cottage, but for the most part, they were recaptured within a few days by police with the aid of black-trackers. Theirs was then the lot of the parti-coloured clothes for runaways, and the dragging chains; and their discomfort struck a note of warning to the rest. But Moondyne Joe was different. No prison walls could hold him long. Only four months ago, Sykes would be told, he had escaped again.

Moondyne Joe — whose real name was Joseph Bolitho Johns — had emigrated as a convict on the *Pyrenees*, arriving on 1 May 1853.[11] He was then aged twenty-two and was five feet eleven inches in height, with black hair, hazel eyes, a long visage, clear-complexioned and of healthy appearance. His trade was that of miner and dresser, and his state single.[12] He already had his ticket of leave when he landed, for the *Pyrenees* had brought only ticket-of-leave men, and he gained his conditional pardon two years later, on 10 March 1855.[13] Free, he went over the hills and lived casually, breaking in horses, and picking up strayed horses for which he received a reward. His method was to build horse-traps at springs where stray horses would come for water. He would watch and confine them, and then produce them for reward. The Toodyay police reported in 1860 and 1861 that Joseph Johns was putting up horse-traps at the Moondyne Springs.[14] Unfortunately for him, however (though it was never proved), it was thought that he often helped the horses to stray, and this at last led to a charge of horse-stealing. While in gaol awaiting trial he broke out, and when recaptured, the charge of horse-stealing was dropped, but he earned three further years' imprisonment for gaol-breaking. He was discharged in 1864. Nine months later, he was back in prison on a ten-year sentence for killing an ox with intent to steal the carcase. This time he absconded from a working party, to be brought back and given a year in irons. He managed to obtain a pick-lock, file and knife and with the latter two made a saw. The lock was nearly cut out of his cell door when he was discovered. Clapped into the refractory cells, in irons, Joe ten days later escaped again. He was free for two months and went back to his old haunts by the Moondyne Springs. 'He knew every inch of the country between the Helena River, the head of the Swan and Chittering Brook,' says one account of him. He knew, in fact, how to live off the country.[15]

There is nothing to show in records of Moondyne Joe the bushranger that he ever had a gun, or stole one. No one was afraid of him: during one of his bursts of freedom while he was ranging the bush around the Upper Swan, the Guildford correspondent of *The Inquirer* shows the lack of worry on the part of the inhabitants by writing in his column:

> The probable whereabouts of Moondyne Joe and his companions, and the consequent imaginary visits to be paid shortly to our surrounding homesteads are topics that have given place to the forthcoming cricket match.[16]

There was good-humoured tolerance of his exploits on the part of the general public, whom he amused; but not on the part of Governor Hampton, whom he did not; for Moondyne's continued escapes brought ridicule on the system.

Governor Hampton had succeeded Governor Kennedy in 1862. His years of experience as Comptroller General of Convicts in Tasmania had made him a strict disciplinarian, and this he continued to be in Western Australia. *The Inquirer*, writing on the subject of convict discipline on 5 September 1866, referred to recent escapes which had become more numerous under Hampton's repressive regime, and spoke of the severity of punishment to those who were recaptured. They could be sentenced by the magistrates to work in irons for one or two years; could receive 100 lashes, and perhaps six to nine months' solitary confinement beginning with fourteen to thirty days' starvation diet (bread and water). Should such absconders' conduct subsequently be satisfactory, their irons could be removed, but they were never allowed to join a road party. The newspaper remarked that those who had fled from country road parties had had but short respite, 'with the exception of that celebrity, Moondyne Joe'.

Moondyne had escaped from the Toodyay gaol, the Perth gaol and the Fremantle Establishment. At large when *The Inquirer* was referring to him as 'that celebrity', he was retaken at the end of September 1866, and was then chained and put into the special strong cell with its caged window. He was given a starvation diet of bread and water to lower his vigorous spirit, and what with this, and the dark and fetid air of his cell, in some months he was in such a state that the prison surgeon strongly recommended that he must have more fresh air or he would die. So each morning, after the other convicts had gone to work, he was taken from his cell and put into a corner of the prison yard, where he could be watched by a sentry.

No one was allowed near him. A heap of stone lay waiting for him to break, which was supposed to be removed at the end of each day; but through some oversight, it was allowed to accumulate and soon was a mount nearly four feet high and eight feet long. Moondyne Joe was never a man to waste his opportunities. By Friday 8 March 1867, he had made his plan.

All that day the sentry could see him swinging his hammer, but could not see the large stone at the bottom of the wall of the prison yard being loosened and smashed, hidden by the rising heap. Joe himself was partially hidden by the heap, so the sentry kept calling, 'Are you there, Joe?' Towards the end of the day, he could just see Joe sitting with his head bent down; and when he did not get any answer to his cry, 'Are you there, Joe?' thought Joe was having forty winks, and kindly let him be. At five o'clock he went over and said. 'Come along now, Joe.' But the seated figure did not stir.[17] The horrified sentry found he was looking at Joe's hat stuck on top of a hammer thrust into the pile of stones, and another hammer crosswise holding out his shirt, while his parti-coloured trousers lay huddled on the ground. Joe himself had flown. Clad in his flannel drawers and boots, he had got through the hole he had made in the wall into the yard of the Superintendent's house, which was built into the outer walls, and had calmly walked out by the Superintendent's front gate.[18]

The signal gun was fired at once. The pensioner guard was called out; parties of warders spread through the streets of Fremantle, and excitement prevailed both in the town and in the prison. Joe had done it again.

This was the joke that Sykes heard when he came. It was considered a very good joke to have played on the Governor, and on his son, Mr G.E. Hampton, who was Acting Comptroller General. The Governor had incurred a good deal of censure by placing his son, who was also his private secretary, in the position of Comptroller General as a temporary measure while awaiting a new officer from England. Mr Hampton's private life was not beyond reproach; he held other public offices as well as that of Comptroller General, and the final touch was added to the colonists' displeasure when the Governor allotted him £100 living allowance, to which he was entitled by regulations but which he did not need as he resided at Government House. Mr Hampton had been zealous in awarding the severest punishments to convict offenders. He had openly exulted in the strong cell he had devised for Moondyne Joe, 'that immense scoundrel', as he called him. The Governor was reputed to have remarked when he saw it: 'If Moondyne can get out of that, I'll forgive him.' Now they were both laughing stocks. All the urchins in Fremantle and in Perth were chanting to a well-known air:[19]

The Governor's son has got the pip,
The Governor's got the measles.
For Moondyne Joe has give 'em the slip.
Pop goes the weasel.[20]

The irritating little tune could still be heard shrilly whistled by passers-by as they went down the street beneath the gaol walls when William Sykes sat in his cell waiting to find out what was to become of him. The end of the story came after Sykes had left the gaol for his assignment. It may, however, have struck some chord in his imagination, for later he was to work at Toodyay not far from the Moondyne Hills and there he was to die.

On this occasion, Moondyne's freedom lasted nearly two years. Then his luck failed him. He came over the hills one dark night to pay a visit to Houghton Vineyard, owned by Mr C.W. Ferguson. He had a kind of fondness for this place: through taking a fancy to one of Mr Ferguson's horses he had done a stretch in gaol. Now he rather fancied some of Mr Ferguson's good wine. Getting into the wine cellar was no trouble at all to a man who could get out of gaols so easily; but unfortunately for him, hard on his heels that night came Mr Ferguson and some mounted troopers, who had been dragging the river nearby for a body. They were cold and wet. It was one o'clock in the morning before they had finished so Ferguson had asked them in for a drink of wine to warm them. Ferguson himself never forgot the happenings of 25 February 1869.

> When I put my key into the lock of the cellar door I found it unlocked and it creaked ajar. I thought it was strange, but concluded that it had not been closed when work had ceased for the day. I therefore lighted a candle I was carrying and commenced to walk along the cellar between the rows of wine barrels. The cellar

was about 60 feet long, and the spluttering flame of the candle did little more than dimly light the few feet in front of me. One of my men was carrying a large jug, and we commenced to walk towards a cask of wine that was on tap. We had only gone a few yards from the door when there was an unearthly yell, and the tall figure of a man, with hair streaming over his shoulders and looking extremely weird, with the contrivance he carried over his head and shoulders, sprang out of the darkness ... He had allowed his hair to grow in long plaits over his shoulders, and he also grew a very long beard. In anticipation of the plunder he expected to carry away with him from the cellars, he had cut a hole in the centre of a wheat sack and fitted it over his head. In each end of the sack he had a two-gallon keg, one in front and one at the back. He had covered his boots with sheep skins to disguise his tracks.[21]

He was also carrying a waddy of tough York gum about two feet long, with which he swung at Mr Ferguson; but the troopers were at hand, and in no time Moondyne Joe was a prisoner again.

Moondyne Joe had the stuff of legend about him, for he captured the imagination, and his nickname was colourful and euphonious. The name Moondyne gave the title to a novel about convict days written by the Fenian prisoner, John Boyle O'Reilly, which, although it had nothing to do with the real Joe, helped to perpetuate the legend of a gallant and notable figure. The real Joe, it cannot be denied, was a bit of a rogue, a man of considerable ingenuity, with a likable personality. The stories about him contain somewhere the seed of truth that has twisted as it has grown. Witness the tale that Joe, escaping, crossed the new bridge over the Swan River at Fremantle the night before it was to be opened by Governor Hampton, who was to drive across it in state. Newspaper accounts of the time show that the bridge had no formal opening. Governor Hampton and his son, the Acting Comptroller General, drove over it for the first time on 14 November 1866, and it was open for traffic on 28 November.[22] As Joe was taken back to prison in September 1866 and did not escape again till March 1867, he could not have forestalled the Governor, unless in proceeding the other way — back to gaol under guard. It is just possible that he was taken over the nearly-finished bridge instead of using the old ferry, and he may have quipped to the police escorting him that he had used the bridge first.[23]

After doing his full sentence at Fremantle under less rigorous conditions with Wakeford as Comptroller General, he was sent down to the Vasse district on ticket of leave. Here he worked at timber-cutting, was apparently well liked by his mates, and gave no further trouble to the authorities.[24] A number of tales about him sprang up in the Vasse district, and some rather poor ballads. He is said to have died in the Old Men's Home at Claremont, Western Australia, in 1920.

The voyage out to Western Australia had been a brief period of reunion for the four poachers, Sykes, Teale, Bone and Bentcliffe. Once arrived at the Convict Establishment, however, their particulars taken and their use for the various public works assessed, they were drafted off to their different assignments. In the early years of the convict period, probation prisoners such as they were — those with some years to serve before gaining their tickets of leave — were kept in the Establishment at work on restricted local projects. In these last years, unless prisoners were classed as 'incorrigibles', they were sent far afield on public works while they were still in their probation stage.

Henry Bone and John Bentcliffe found themselves sailing northward to Champion Bay, a district which had become increasingly important since the discovery of minerals such as lead and copper by the explorer, A.C. Gregory, in 1848, and since his brother F.T. Gregory's explorations had shown that there was good cattle country even farther north. There Bone and Bentcliffe laboured in the sand-drifts that constantly encroached on the growing town of Geraldton. It is unlikely that they ever saw Sykes again. They were due for their tickets of leave in 1874. As for Sykes himself, he and Teale were sent in the opposite direction, southward to Bunbury, to work on road-making.

After one of the periodic complaints from the colonists that the labour of 6,000 convicts had been almost exclusively devoted to the erection of buildings for the convicts themselves and of very handsome residences for the officers, when it might have been used more on public works, and especially on roads, Captain Henderson was moved to reply, somewhat peevishly and rather inaccurately: 'It seems to be forgotten, that although Western Australia had been in existence twenty-one years by 1850, there were not then five miles of cleared road in the colony.'[25]

'As regards the road from Perth to King George's Sound,' he continued:

> I can only say that it is my opinion that any expenditure thereon, except as is absolutely necessary for the mail cart, is a waste. The road traverses a line of country utterly useless and uninhabitable; it opens up nothing and is scarcely used by anyone except the mail-man.

At this date the mail steamers from England called at Albany, not Fremantle, and the English mails were sent overland to Perth by coach, taking from four to five days on the bad road.

In defending the amount of road-work done by his convicts, Captain Henderson exaggerated when he said there were not five miles of cleared road when he and they came to the colony. A road of sorts from King George's Sound to the capital had been in continuous use since April 1841, when a monthly overland mail to Albany had been established.[26] From even earlier years, the settlers of Augusta, Busselton and Bunbury had used a track that ran straight up the coast a few miles inland, passing by the ill-fated Australind settlement,[27] through paper-bark swamps and peppermint forests, by the dreaming waters of the Harvey Estuary and Peel Inlet, and by Mandurah northward to Fremantle. Over the hills, a road to York established before 1838 had been kept in repair partly at the expense of the York settlers, partly by a toll at Mahogany Creek, and partly by the rather feeble efforts of the General Road Trust, which was responsible for roads before the coming of the convicts.

The *Perth Gazette* had published a very critical letter on 30 January 1847, referring to the management of public roads. It said that in 'this ill-managed colony' the Government should, after a proper examination of the country, have fixed upon the great lines of communication to every settled district, and formed and maintained the roads. The main roads were the chance tracks of early settlers; and even when the Government did order a line of road to be marked out — who did it? The Government Residents of each district, with imperfect means at their disposal. As a consequence, scarcely a line of road existed which might not be greatly improved and shortened. For this it blamed the General Road Trust, which it called 'a fluctuating, irresponsible body'. The Trust consisted of a chairman, treasurer, clerk and committee, and the Directors of Districts. The latter were the Resident Magistrates and three or four prominent settlers of each district.[28]

The Road Trust itself blamed the Survey Department which it said was occupied in:

> laying out theoretical town-sites never likely to have an inhabitant, instead of the practical business of marking roads, and laying down on maps the actual position of existing homesteads, so as to enable the settlers to lay out communications in the best line.[29]

The Survey Department, meanwhile, was having trouble trying to re-survey the boundary lines of established farms, the owners of which were generally unwilling to part with any of their land that might lie within an intended line of road.

By the time the convicts came in 1850, therefore, there were hundreds of miles of roughly cleared tracks radiating from Perth northward to Victoria Plains, south to Bunbury and Augusta, south-east to the Williams River and Albany, and due east to York, Northam and Toodyay. They were tracks, however, that became almost impassable in winter and many were axle-deep in sand in the summer. What was so vitally needed was roads with good stone foundations, macadamized roads (though the term as then used did not imply a sealed road, but only a road made according to the principles of Macadam, with successive layers of broken stone and a smooth top layer) and roads that had water available for man and beast. Many of the early lines were not direct because they had to pass by springs and streams. Wells at approximately every ten miles along the different tracks were among the first works of the convicts.

Work on roads and bridges progressed too slowly for the colonists' liking until the advent of Governor Hampton. That worthy pursued a vigorous policy of public works, particularly with regard to roads. Like Macadam, he even gave his name to a type of road: on the sandy coastal plain around Perth, where the only stone was soft limestone, the road to Fremantle, the road to Wanneroo and the road to Green Mount were based with 'Governor Hampton's Cheeses' — round sections of tough jarrah, that made a good firm foundation in the sand.[30] When Hampton had received notice in 1865 of the British Government's decision to discontinue transportation after 1867, he had determined to make the most of the last years in which public works could be performed at the Home Government's expense. In these last two years, 1,660 convicts were landed, and were largely dispersed on road-making. Harsh disciplinarian Hampton may have been, but he achieved results; the colonists were sorry to see him go when his term of office expired, and tried to have it prolonged by means of a monster petition to the Secretary of State for the Colonies, but without success. Hampton left the colony on 2 November 1868.

While Bone and Bentcliffe had sailed for Champion Bay, Sykes and Teale, together with sixteen other convicts, in the charge of one warder, embarked on a small sailing ship, the *Wild Wave*, 28 tons, Edward Pettit, master, bound for Bunbury and the Vasse. The ship carried a cargo of three cases of brandy, twenty-one packages of merchandise under bond, thirty bags of sugar, twenty-seven and a half chests of tea, 104 packages and cases of sundries.[31] A number of small boats of about this tonnage plied up and down the coast, as far south as Albany and as far north as Port Gregory.

The port of Bunbury, about a hundred miles south of Fremantle, was at this time in a flourishing condition. It had a good jetty a quarter of a mile long. Ships loading timber for Mauritius and sleepers for India, as well as horses, wool, and sandalwood, put in there. It was a favourite resort of American whalers at certain seasons of the year, when there might be as many as eleven vessels in the bay at once. The American seamen came on shore with plenty of American money which was accepted as good currency in Bunbury. Barter and exchange of commodities went on, and the local inhabitants derived a good deal of harmless amusement from the efforts of the Americans to ride horses while on shore. It goes without saying that the hosts of the Swan Inn and the Plough and Harrow, the Wellington Hotel and the Rose Hotel, were always pleased when the whalers were in. The town authorities were not so pleased, however. The officers of the Convict Depot and the police had to be constantly on the alert at such times, for there was always the chance that prisoners might manage to escape by means of an American ship. Some escapes did occur, but the whalers' price was high, and not many convicts, even ticket-of-leave men, could raise the money to get away by them.

The town of Bunbury was neatly laid out and showed more progress than the neighbouring and older town of Busselton, a little farther south down the coast. Bunbury had been one of the first places to have a hiring-station for ticket-of-leave men set up soon after the convicts had landed in the colony. Besides the depot and warders' quarters, there were a convict hospital and commissariat buildings, a court house and gaol, and police quarters. Pensioners' cottages with well-tilled gardens added to the size and appearance of the town. There were several churches and quite a few stores. The main street had good foot-paths and was well made. It needed to be, with the bullock wagons loaded high with sandalwood and wool trundling down it to the jetty.

Much fine country had recently been opened up inland from Bunbury, in the neighbourhood of the upper reaches of the Blackwood River; but the tracks — for they could not be called roads — leading to it through forests thickly timbered with magnificent tall trees became quite impassable during the winter rains. Since the season was now approaching when the wool from the inland farms had to be taken to Bunbury to be shipped, the way had to be cleared for the bullock teams and Hester's Bridge, which had been washed away, had to be repaired. Other bridges needed to be built. Road parties had already been working on this line when Sykes and the other convicts arrived in Bunbury. They had no time to see anything of the town before they were despatched to reinforce the working parties on the Blackwood road.[32] At this time, 1867, the district around Bunbury, known as Wellington, had ninety-eight convicts dispersed on public works in it. Thereafter the numbers decreased.[33]

To be put on a country road party was a condition of convict life infinitely preferable to any other part of it. A party usually consisted of from twenty to forty men in the charge of a warder, who administered it under control from the nearest Convict Depot. The men lived in huts or tents according to the climate and the length of time they would be stationed at a particular place. The huts were of brushwood or slab, roofed with paper-bark or blackboy rushes. The life was reasonably free of discipline, and although they worked nine hours a day, after work for the day was over it was pleasant to saunter about the clearing round the huts, or sit around the campfire and yarn, eat savoury kangaroo or cockatoo stew, and drink hot pannikins of fragrant billy tea. Some of the prisoners made pets of possums or parrots; no dogs were allowed to be kept at road stations. There was little misbehaviour, and though the warder in charge had a gun, he was seldom called upon to use it. Indeed, in some cases the warder simply drew a line in perimeter of the huts and announced that beyond this the men might not go. The main trouble was from passing travellers, who sometimes supplied prisoners with liquor. A Circular to Magistrates issued early in 1859 urged them to enforce the law rigorously against such persons, as 'much mischief and disgrace have arisen therefrom'.[34]

The warder in charge usually had a convict constable to assist him in keeping order. These were men who had behaved with conspicuous good conduct and so had been promoted to the role of constable. Such promotion carried with it a gratuity beyond what ordinary convicts were allowed to earn per day. Ordinary convicts could earn from 1d. to $2^1/_4$d. per day according to behaviour, while constables received 1s. per day after three months' service. After six months they got 1s. 6d. per day, and after twelve months, 2s. 6d. per day. (This money was held by the Convict Department for the prisoner and paid in a lump sum to him when he left on ticket of leave.) They were also eligible for increased remission of sentence, while a man who had served as a First Class constable for eighteen months could be recommended for appointment to the colonial police force. The constable system proved to work quite well under these inducements, not to speak of a further one: constables did not have to have their hair cut short, and they could grow whiskers, if they so desired.[35]

Although most convicts liked the life on road parties, there were always some who did not. It was no rare occurrence for the inhabitants of Bunbury to see a police constable and his swarthy assistant, a black-tracker clad only in a 'boka', or short kangaroo-skin cloak, riding into town accompanied by convicts who had absconded from their party and had been retaken in the bush by their pursuers. Sometimes such absconders made for the sea and tried to get aboard a vessel, only to be caught. These foolhardy attempts earned them three years' imprisonment with or without flogging, in the chain gang back at Fremantle gaol. In November 1868, three convicts escaped from the depot and tried to take possession of the cutter *Wild Wave* which was anchored out. The captain, who had been warned, was lying in wait for them and hailed the police, who were also waiting, and that was the end of that attempt.[36] But another better planned affair, which depended on outside help, was more successful.

The last ship ever to bring convicts to Australia, the *Hougoumont*, which had followed the *Norwood*, had brought, among others, sixty-two Fenian prisoners, one of whom was John Boyle O'Reilly. By deliberate design, the Fenians were dispersed all over the colony, and O'Reilly was one of those sent down to Bunbury early in 1868. The convicts from the *Hougoumont* were put to work on a new route laid out from Bunbury to the Vasse that avoided most of the sandy country through which the old road had passed.[37] O'Reilly spent a year working in this district. It gave him the material for many poems in later years, and the background, considerably, in fact almost unrecognizably altered by imagination, for his novel, *Moondyne*. Like Sykes, O'Reilly would have heard of the exploits of the real Moondyne Joe during his brief period in Fremantle gaol, before being sent to Bunbury.

Unlike many of his fellow Irishmen all over Australia,

O'Reilly wanted no part of this new country. He only wanted to leave it as quickly as possible. O'Reilly enlisted the sympathies of Father McCabe, the Roman Catholic priest of the parish of Bunbury, who helped him to escape. Father McCabe, with the assistance of a settler named Maguire who lived at nearby Dardanup, where there was a little settlement of free Irish people, made arrangements with the captain of an American whaler, the *Vigilant* from New Bedford, to take O'Reilly on to his vessel. It was easy enough for O'Reilly to leave his camp on the Vasse road, but to get out to the *Vigilant* was another matter. Maguire had arranged for a small boat to be hidden along the coast a little north of Bunbury, and he and O'Reilly rowed out towards the *Vigilant* when she set sail from the bay. The *Vigilant* belied her name, however, for she passed the little craft without noticing it, and sailed away. O'Reilly had to return to shore and hide for over a week until Father McCabe and James Maguire were able to make other arrangements with another whaler, the *Gazelle*. This time the effort was successful. O'Reilly went on board the *Gazelle*, was transhipped to another American vessel, the *Sapphire*, at the Cape of Good Hope, and eventually landed at Liverpool. From there, he took a passage to Boston, where he became a respected citizen, the editor of a newspaper, the *Pilot*, and the writer of many works of somewhat dubious literary merit.[38] Other Irishmen, bond and free, had remained where he fled, to add their blood and effort to the new country.

Some of O'Reilly's fellow Fenians had to wait another seven years before outside influence could arrange their escape. Six of them were 'rescued' in 1876 through the instrumentality of an American, John Collins, a prominent Fenian, who had arranged with an American whaler, the *Catalpa*, to be off the Western Australian coast in April of that year to take the Fenians on board. Collins had been in Fremantle for some time beforehand, and had made all the arrangements for the men's escape from that town. Not until they had boarded a whale-boat from the *Catalpa* in the vicinity of Rockingham, seventeen miles down the coast south of Fremantle, was the alarm given, and then there was considerable delay before a police boat put out from Fremantle in search of them. The government steamer *Georgette* also put out from the port and hailed the *Catalpa*, and was told no convicts were on board. The *Georgette* then returned to Fremantle, but the police boat delayed and saw the whale-boat approach the *Catalpa* from the south and the men taken on board. Returning to Fremantle as fast as possible the police reported to the Governor, who ordered the *Georgette* to sea again, this time armed with a 12-lb. artillery piece. An exciting chase took place. The *Georgette* overtook the *Catalpa* off Rottnest Island, fired a shot across her bows, and demanded the escaped prisoners. Although three of the Fenians could be seen hanging over the rail grinning, the captain denied that he had any but seamen on board. The Superintendent of Water Police threatened to fire at the ship, but the captain with a dramatic gesture pointed to the American flag flying aloft and roared: 'This flag protects me!' Cramming on all sails, the *Catalpa* then stood away, and the *Georgette* had to return to Fremantle.[39] The populace of Western Australia was very indignant about all this; but Governor Robinson in a despatch to the Colonial Office, while he admitted that there had been bungling on the part of the police authorities who had allowed the *Georgette* to put to sea without sufficient fuel to chase the *Catalpa* when it had first sighted her off Rockingham, was quite patently glad that the Fenians had quitted the shores of Western Australia to become the problem of some other nation.[40] None of the Australian colonies wanted Fenians and tried to prevent those with expired sentences from entering.[41]

William Sykes and John Teale must have found it hard to settle down to camp life in the dense bush of the Blackwood road. The trees were the tallest they had ever seen, rising sometimes 200 feet before the first branch sprang. It was like living in a land of oppressive giants who loomed over pygmy men labouring frantically with ineffectual axes and saws below. The summer sun penetrated the high tree tops to fall in slanting lines down to the thick prickly scrub and bracken fern, from which rose a humid heat and swarms of tiny insects. Clouds of flies clung to men's backs and the sticky sweat of their faces, getting into their nostrils and eyes. Shrieking parrots mocked them. In many ways the bush manifested its hostility, and the contrast of its space and freedom to the confined existence they had been leading placed a terrible mental strain on them. Back in camp at night, Sykes and Teale could take their turn at tales around the campfire, but when they lay on their bush beds, scenes from home would rush in comparison before their closed eyelids, and they would shiver to hear the noises of the alien night outside the hut. The harsh chorus of bullfrogs in the swamps would drag them back from their native Yorkshire; if the frogs were still, it was worse, for then could be heard a silence so deep that it had a sound of its own, a far sound of silence echoing over limitless bush.

They could not stand it. They had come from the outskirts of the large city of Sheffield: they had to get to a town again, to see people, and hear the noise of laughter and ribald song from taverns; above all, go where there were lights in windows and open doorways. After three months of bush life, even the few lights of Bunbury enticed them. Not in any attempt to escape, they left the camp and made their way back to Bunbury.

Needless to say, they were soon picked up again. Their records were marked: 'Mutinous and insubordinate conduct leaving camp and returning to Bunbury'.[42] They were given two months' gang labour and their tobacco ration was stopped for six months. They were lucky to get off so lightly. They could have been punished with solitary confinement on bread and water in Bunbury gaol, with a few lashes thrown in, had Mr Hampton still been Comptroller General.

Life in the bush must have prompted William Sykes to think of home. In July of the next year he wrote his first letter to England. Convicts were allowed to write a letter every three months, and the amount of postage was charged against their gratuity earnings and marked on the prison register. His letter cost Sykes 6d. and the record shows that he wrote once in 1868, twice in 1869, and once in 1870. It was, of course, possible that he sent other letters not through the Convict Department, but this is unlikely, for he would have had no money for postage. It was an offence for prisoners to be in possession of money. Teale's record shows that in 1875 he was in possession of 1s. 6d., which was forfeited.

The letter posted in July must have reached England quickly, and brought an immediate answer to the lonely man in the bush (Toodyay Letter No. 5). This gave him news of friends and mentioned all the old familiar names. He learned that his daughter Ann, now aged fourteen, was in service and doing well; and Alfred, aged eleven, was working in a mill for 10d. per day. They had all moved to lodgings four doors up the street. The arrangement was evidently not satisfactory, for in the next letter Myra wrote that she had gone back to live in Greasbrough (Toodyay Letter No. 6). This letter was written a year later and shows that in that year, 1869, Sykes had written only to his sister and not to his wife, for she gently reproaches him with it. Myra addressed this letter: For William Sykes, 9589 Bombrey Depot, Westren Australia [sic]. On the back of the envelope (which is one of those that have disappeared) was written in red ink, presumably by some official: Harvey Road Party, Bunbury Depot.

After the excursion to Bunbury together, Sykes and Teale appear to have been separated, although both remained in the Bunbury district. It was probably better for Sykes to lose Teale's companionship, for Teale was evidently a man of violent temper. In June 1868, he was imprisoned in the gaol at Bunbury and put on bread and water for seven days for cruelly beating a horse with which he had been working on a road party. After that, he was attached to a survey party, and while employed on survey had some kind of accident, which earned him a remission of three months' gang labour. It may also have left him weakened or incapacitated to some degree, for from then onwards, his record shows remissions for good conduct and 'clemency'.

Sykes, meanwhile, was on the Harvey Road party. This party made extensive repairs to fourteen miles of road, raising it in many parts, for the district was very swampy; cutting six miles of drain and putting in eight large and several small culverts.[43] From there, he returned to Bunbury to be sent to work on the Capel Bridge in August 1871. He had written to his wife in July 1870, but for a long while he did not hear from her. The letter, when it came, was only dated 9 March, the year not given; but from comparison with the rest of the letters and from the slight data in it, it was probably written in 1872 (Toodyay Letter No. 7). In the interval since Myra's letter of 1869, Ann had married and had had a child. In giving the family news, Myra reveals a sadness and hopelessness she had not shown before, particularly in the last pitiful words.

# CHAPTER 5

# Over the Hills

To be on Warder Burton's road party was to be one of a crack team, if such a term could be applied to a gang of convicts. Warder Burton's party had made themselves a name for good bridge-building in the Wellington district; but as well as earning a worthy reputation with the settlers, the convicts earned themselves remission of sentence for good work. William Sykes was one of Burton's party from August 1871, when he worked on the Capel Bridge, to 1874, by which time the party was back on the Harvey Road. In September 1874 Sykes and the rest of the party were sent back to Fremantle, not through any midemeanours but as a result of a change in the convict system.

The cessation of transportation had caused the British Government to curtail its expenditure in Western Australia, and as a measure of economy the Comptroller General, Mr Wakeford, recommended to the Governor the closing of various country convict depots, and the drawing-in of outlying parties of convicts. Albany was the first whose closing was recommended, on 2 February 1872. The twenty-four convicts in the depot there were to be transferred to Fremantle for distribution to other work. The buildings of the depot were to be handed over to the Colonial Government, and the stores, furniture and tools were to be sold.[1]

Champion Bay in the north was the next to go. At this depot there were forty-one imperial convicts and twenty-nine colonial; the imperial convicts only, with their officers, were to be returned to Fremantle. On 16 February a further memorandum from Wakeford to the Governor recommended that the depot at Newcastle be closed, and its men sent either to York or to Guildford depot, while the buildings were to be handed over to the Colonial Government. The convicts at the Vasse depot were to be transferred to Bunbury.[2]

This measure brought protests from all over the colony. The Resident Magistrate of the Vasse wrote to the Colonial Secretary a long letter ending:

> I will not further remark except that however rotten the support given to the colony by these men has been, they had done an immense amount of work on our roads and in our towns. The sudden withdrawal of the depot will, I unhesitatingly state, have a depressing effect upon the settlers. I would therefore hope that His Excellency will allow it to remain at any rate, for twelve months longer.[3]

A public meeting was called in Perth for 17 April, at which

Mr S. Burges of York, supported by other landowners from over the hills, proposed a resolution urging the Governor to keep open the country depots, for great hardship would result to settlers if the depots were broken up. These protests did little good, although the depots of York and Bunbury were retained until 1874. From the settlers' point of view the depots were necessary not only as centres of probation prisoners for working parties, but as centres where ticket-of-leave men were registered and from which they could be hired as labour.

The years from 1872 to 1874 were a transition period in the working of the convict system, which had become cumbrous and expensive as fewer and fewer convicts remained in the charge of the Convict Department. Administration machinery that had been built up had to be retracted and diminished. As well as the concentration of prisoners at Fremantle gaol in 1872 in the interests of economy, the office of Comptroller General was dispensed with, Mr Wakeford was transferred by the Colonial Office, and a temporary Acting Comptroller General installed. The Colonial Office passed on to Governor Weld for consideration a series of recommendations by Colonel Du Cane, who had by now become Inspector-General of Military Prisons, and Chairman of the Board of Directors of Convict Prisons in England, for the cutting down of costs and the transference of other costs to the Colonial Government; and the Governor appointed a board to study the subjects proposed, the board consisting of the Colonial Secretary, the Acting Comptroller General, and the Control Officer-in-Charge, all three formerly composing the finance board for convict matters.[4]

In an attempt to convey what the restriction of imperial expenditure would mean to the colony, Governor Weld wrote to the Earl of Kimberley, Secretary of State for the Colonies:

> I do trust, my Lord, that you will bear in mind that this unfortunate colony has lost much in one sense by the introduction of convicts, lost again in another by the cessation of transportation, has not received the equivalent she had reason to expect when she sold her honour and is now struggling for existence under the pressure of the hand of Providence weighing on her in continued bad seasons, floods and tempests, whilst she has out of her poverty to support criminals, lunatics and paupers — the dregs of the cup she has drained.[5]

The decision of the British Government that the colony must pay for pauper convicts and those too sick or infirm to support themselves was indeed a hard one. 'It has already been proposed in the Legislature by a popular member to ship off the ex-convict paupers to England,' wrote Weld. This was taken by the Colonial Office to be a jest, but it was probably semi-serious, and mentioned by Weld to show how local feeling was running. The British Government also proposed to cut down the payment towards the maintenance of the police force. This had always been two-thirds of the cost of the force. As the Convict Department dwindled, however, it was necessary to increase the size of the police force to control the growing number of ticket-of-leave and conditional release men at large in the community, and a

139

reduction of Britain's contribution would be keenly felt by the Colonial Government. Agreement was finally reached that the amount contributed towards the maintenance of the police department should decrease annually until twenty years after the cessation of transportation, when it would cease altogether, most of the convicts from whom trouble could be expected being dead or incapable of harm by then.

Many of the former convict depot buildings which had been handed over to the Colonial Government (although without any formal transfer) were converted into police stations, court houses, residences for magistrates and medical officers, and hospitals, during this period of transition.[6] The settlers were satisfied to find that the hiring of labour remained much as before: ticket-of-leave and conditional release men registered at the magistrate's office, agreements with settlers as to type and terms of work were also registered there; and the police stations, with more mounted constables and native assistants, kept a vigilant watch on the districts.

After seven years of working on the roads in the Wellington district, William Sykes on his return to Fremantle found himself among a select few. At this stage, 1874, there were only 324 probation and re-convicted men left, for whom employment had to be found during the next few years before they got their tickets of leave.[7] Sykes's ticket was due on 28 October 1878, according to his record, but he had already earned several months' remission.

Although his record does not show it, there is reason to believe that he was sent from Fremantle to Toodyay — or as it was named at that period, Newcastle — about October 1875.

He was certainly there on ticket of leave in 1877; ticket-of-leave men were allowed a certain amount of choice with regard to the district to which they would be registered, and they usually chose one they had worked in, or knew. Among the Toodyay letters is an envelope addressed to William Sykes, Newcastle, West Australia, with the date stamp, Rotherham, E, Ja 19, 76. As the envelope is not re-addressed by officials, Sykes must have been in Newcastle at least three months before January 1876, and possibly longer, for his family to have received his address from him and posted him a letter by that date.

There had been a long gap in Sykes's correspondence between 1870 and 1874. No postage appears on his record between those years, and his wife's next letter, of 1875 (Toodyay Letter No. 8), reveals that no one had heard from him for a long time, so long that they supposed him to be dead. 'I put the chealdren and my self in black for you my little Tirza went to the first place in deap black,' she wrote, but her pain could not reach the heart of William Sykes. England was far away, and the life he was living, in the company of other dull and brutish men, occupied his thoughts and feelings.

On leaving Fremantle prison, Sykes would have travelled over the hills to Toodyay on foot, possibly with a party of ticket-of-leave men going there to seek work. Five days' rations was the amount awarded for the journey. Although the distance was but sixty-three miles, twenty miles a day might be considered a fair march. Where the distances were not too far, convict travel was always by foot, to save expense. Only invalids were sent by cart, usually mail cart, from outlying districts to the capital if they were very sick or infirm. The cost from Toodyay to Perth for such a person was £1 1s. 0d.[8]

The way led through Perth to Guildford. About three miles past Guildford the road forked, one branch going up what was called the 'York Green Mount', and on over the hills to York by a line of road originally known as 'King Dick's Line'.[9] The other branch wound roughly parallel with the ranges before ascending them at what was known as the 'Toodyay Green Mount'. Both these ascents were steep, and as they had needed maintenance for the teams from over the hills, there had been road stations at each from the earliest convict days. Lieutenant Du Cane, in charge of the Guildford depot, reported in 1854:

> On the Toodyay road about six miles from hence, a station has been erected capable of containing 60 men, a room for the sick, a cookhouse, a warder's quarters, and a quarter and store room for the assistant superintendent; these buildings are of mud, with thatched roofs, the timber in the vicinity not being so well adapted to making slabhouses as on the York Road.
>
> On the York road, about six miles from this, has been erected a station consisting of a Ticket-of-leave men's barracks capable of holding 70 men, a cookhouse containing oven and fireplace, houses for the assistant superintendent, the instructing warder, and stores.
>
> It is proposed to erect several such stations as these in suitable spots along the roads for the accommodation

of working parties on the road, or for resting places for the drafts of men going up the country from Fremantle.[10]

Although the York and Toodyay Green Mount road stations were no longer in use for road parties by 1875, it is probable they were still used as overnight stops by men going up-country. If William Sykes slept at Toodyay Green Mount he would have found the group of mud huts still in tolerable repair. Later, as the thatched roofs rotted and tumbled, they became derelict, but the mud walls remained, more and more ruined, as late as 1928. Those on the York road, at what was known as the Darlington turn-off, thereafter disintegrated rapidly as more and more motor traffic on that road brought more people to kick them down. The main buildings on the Toodyay road remained recognizable longer, and one or two fragments of corners and fireplaces are still visible today on Redhill, formerly Toodyay Green Mount.

The Toodyay road was a lonely road, steep, gravelly and well-watered. It had been a track to Toodyay at least since 1841, although one of the first tasks of the road parties had been to alter the Toodyay end of the track by cutting a new line of road there, to avoid the heavy ascent of Jimpeting Hill. The diary for 1841 of a young Irishman, Henry de Burgh, describes his route:

On the 30th December I took an excursion to the Toodyay with Sam Phillips — He was taking a load and experienced great difficulty in getting up Green

Mount — the entire trip was a series of misfortunes. We got the cart stuck in a valley at the 'Warraloo' where Phillips left me with the cart and horse and rode home to send a fresh team — Never did I feel so hot a day. I attempted to bathe in a pool among the rocks but came out in a second black with leeches. I had a bottle of brandy and some bread and cheese, and under the shelter of the cart reclined, I ushered in the year 1842. The next day I got help and that evening late I reached Phillips' farm. There is a tremendous hill called the 'Jimpeting'. I have seen nothing more steep in any country except perhaps the hill behind Simonstown. I remained a few days here and lived entirely on bronze winged pigeons — indeed nothing could be better. We eat them stewed, with a great deal of gravy — they are larger and I think much better than grouse.[11]

The rural delights of Henry de Burgh were not for William Sykes. He would have had to forgo the pigeons, unless their party had a policeman with them with a rifle. After his days on the Blackwood road Sykes would be used to camping. The day's long march was to be preferred to the high walls of Fremantle gaol, but it may not have been with any feelings of pleasure that he neared Toodyay, his journey's end.

Toodyay was one of the oldest settlements in the colony. In August 1830, Ensign Dale had led an expedition consisting of Mr W.L. Brockman, a soldier and a storekeeper, over the Darling Ranges, in the course of which the site of York was

144

explored and Mount Bakewell named. They found 'a country well clothed with grass, apparently of the same description as that on the banks of the Swan'. Some of the more adventurous settlers at Swan River, hungry for more land, decided to take it up in this country over the hills. In 1831, therefore, Ensign Dale, accompanied by a larger party — Messrs Clarkson and Hardey, George Fletcher Moore and several other gentlemen, and Ensign Dale's servant, a soldier named Sheridan — set off to cross the ranges again, to explore both north and south of Mount Bakewell.

The soldier Sheridan was the life of the party. 'Morning or evening, wet or dry, busy or idle, Sheridan whistled or sang incessantly,' says Moore in his Journal.

It was his duty to wheel a perambulator (an instrument for measuring distances) and off he started with it, singing with stentorian voice the old drum beat: 'Tither, row dow, dow, dow; and tither, ither, row dow, tither ither row dow.'[12]

After reaching Mount Bakewell, they proceeded NNW and after several days came upon a large and beautiful valley. 'This elevated our spirits again,' says Moore. "Worcestershire," cried one; "Shropshire," cried another; "Kilkenny for ever," roared out Sheridan.' The Avon River, whose course they had been following, now began to appear to them as a continuation of the Swan. In this they were right, but the name, Avon, was retained. The valley itself had the native name of Toodyay. As the spelling of native names was phonetic, Toodyay is found in early diaries and letters with

145

several variations — Toogey, Toodyee, Toodyoy and Toodyay.

Settlement followed; in 1837 Alfred Waylen applied for the fee simple of his grant 'on the Toodyee'. This grant was later bought, about 1839, by Samuel Pole Phillips, who settled on it and named his dwelling Culham after his family home in Oxfordshire. In the next decade a town-site to be called Toodyay was planned and laid down on a bend of the Avon River. The plan, made by Alfred Hillman, Assistant Surveyor, in October 1849, looks well on paper, its streets neatly squared and named after governors and statesmen; but, with the river surrounding the site on three sides, it bears an ominous comment: 'flooded during the Survey'.[13] Although the town-site was proceeded with according to this plan, it proved a bad situation. Year after year, the Avon came down in flood, and in some years a great deal of damage was suffered.

Some two miles higher up the river, a grant of land 45 acres 1 rood 20 perches in extent was set apart for Convict Department purposes, about the end of 1851. In August 1851 Governor Fitzgerald advised the Colonial Office that as the convict ship *Pyrenees* had arrived in the winter, before there was adequate accommodation in Fremantle for the number of men on her, they had been sent to the rural districts so that they might be taken into service at once. The necessity for depots in these places had been felt for some time.[14]

A depot and hiring-station at Toodyay was therefore proceeded with immediately, to the subsequent vexation of the Surveyor-General, who wrote to the Colonial Secretary in Perth on 13 June 1853:

Having recently furnished for transmission to England various tracings of Military, Commissariat and Convict Lands, including several for the registration or entry of which in the Record Books of this office no authority has hitherto been officially communicated under sanction of His Excellency the Governor — I have the honour to enclose for His Excellency's approval traced plans of several pieces of land of this description which have for some time past been appropriated to their respective uses under verbal sanction only, and have not hitherto been included in my official Land Returns ...[15]

Among these verbally ordered appropriations he lists: 'No. 5 — Part of Avon district showing 45a 1r 20p set apart for convict purposes on the river Avon above Toodyay townsite.'

He was correct in saying the grant had been in use for some time past, for the Convict Department Return of Buildings shows that the Toodyay depot rapidly became quite a settlement, even if most irregularly, from the Surveyor-General's point of view. A Commissariat store and quarters, warders' quarters, overseer's quarters, and blacksmith's shop were erected between 1851 and 1853; a thirty-foot well was put in, and a depot for sixty men, a hospital, cook-house and bake-house were in progress. The depot was in the charge of a civilian superintendent assisted by one or two instructing warders of the Royal Sappers and Miners.[16]

The convict grant sloped gently upwards from the river bank to a line of granite hills covered with jamwood, wattle and blackboys. Cottages for sappers and miners and their families were built on the upper slope; and in 1852 the Government sent its Assistant Surveyor, F.T. Gregory, to survey lots for pensioners on either side of the grant.[17] An area for church land was also surveyed, but no land for the church itself.

This caused great vexation to Archdeacon Wollaston, a reverend gentleman who had emigrated to Western Australia with the Australind settlers in 1841. A busy, gossipy, endearing little man, he had laboured for the sound establishment of the Church of England in the colony, had been created Archdeadon in 1849, and used to make 300-mile archidiaconal tours on horseback from his own parish at Albany up through the settled districts in the south, to York and Toodyay north of Perth. Observing the progress of the Convict Depot at Toodyay, it irked him to find that he had to preach there to a congregation of convicts, officials, and free settlers all assembled in a tent! He and the chaplain of the district, the Reverend Charles Harper, drew up a plan for converting a stone commissariat store on the convict grant into a church by the addition of a nave, and on 23 March 1853, he submitted the plan to Governor Fitzgerald. The Governor apparently approved of it. 'At least he made no objection', wrote Wollaston in his Journal. 'After I had left him, however, I found the Comptroller General had at once rejected it. As an encroachment, I suppose, on the Convict grant.'[18]

Wollaston had reason to be testy. He considered that the bad influence which the influx of convicts might have on the community ought to be offset by more churches and more chaplains. The Convict Department certainly allowed £50 per annum to the colonial chaplains for their services to the various depots; but Wollaston thought the chaplains' primary duty to the settlers would not be fulfilled unless places were set apart where both convicts and free men might conveniently assemble. The Comptroller General was of the opinion that one of the convict wards at Toodyay depot would do for Divine Service. If this were to be the case, Wollaston thought that chaplains ought to confine themselves to week-day services for the convicts, so that on Sunday the free settlers could have their own service. He continued to battle for a church at Toodyay, but not until after his death was one built. It may have amused his quizzical shade to observe that the church was then erected on part of the convict grant, which was further encroached on and diminished as it became the centre of a new town.

Wollaston died in 1856. In 1857 the River Avon came down in flood and swamped the town-site of Toodyay, while further up river the Convict Depot was high and dry. The flood waters merely shaved off a little of the river banks. The same thing happened again in 1859. By this time the depot and its buildings were almost deserted, because Governor Kennedy had closed down the country hiring-stations for ticket-of-leave men in the interests of economy. (The colonists found ticket-of-leave labour plentiful but expensive: they had to pay the same rate as to free labourers, so when a particular job was done, they tended to return the ticket-of-leave holders to the depot where the Convict Department had to maintain them.) By the end of 1859, only one warder remained at Toodyay to send on returning men to Guildford depot.

Because of the many buildings left there, and the obvious advantages of the site, new surveys were made in 1860 and 1861 around the convict grant, and the grant itself was subdivided into many smaller lots. On 20 August 1861, the Governor and Executive Council approved a new town-site created around the grant, to be called Newcastle, after the Secretary of State for the Colonies, Henry Pelham-Clinton, Lord Lincoln, Duke of Newcastle. His names were given to the streets of the town.[19] The old name of Toodyay still clung to the place, however, and it is sometimes hard to distinguish, apart from official papers, whether references are made to the old or the new town. The new town kept the official name of Newcastle until 1910, when it was changed to Toodyay, and the old town-site, or what remained of it, became West Toodyay.[20]

An influx of 893 convicts into the colony in 1862, allied with Governor Hampton's intention to press on with road-building, caused the reopening of Toodyay, or Newcastle depot was it now was, with the difference that the depot now held probation prisoners assigned to public works and road-making and mending. The Newcastle road to Guildford and Perth was kept in good repair and was regarded as one of the finest roads in the colony.

When Sykes reached Newcastle in 1875, the town was not large. It appeared as a cleared hillside of the Toodyay valley, with a well-made road following the line of the river. Prominent on the hillside were the red brick buildings of the depot, with a few scattered houses standing in paddocks sown for hay. On the river road — the New Road, as it was called then, because it was the new line on to the old Toodyay road — stood a long timber building with a shingled roof, probably a public house; the Road Board building erected in 1874; the Catholic church at one end of the incipient town, and the Church of England, St Stephen's, at the other, near a good jarrah bridge which spanned the river and gave access to the old town and continued north to Culham and Victoria Plains.

Around Newcastle lay handsome properties — Hawthornden, the homestead of James Drummond, the noted botanist; Knockdomny, originally built by Captain Whitfield and later divided between his two sons, the second portion being named Wicklow Hills; Deepdale, the grant of Lionel Lukin; Dumbarton, belonging to James Sinclair; the Clarkson estate of Mr Anderson, and others, all established in the early forties. On the sheep runs they employed many shepherds, for the grants were not fenced in until later; and because of this the sheep were belled. The sound of sheep bells on the evening air was a familiar sound in early Toodyay. The bells were attached to yokes usually made of sandalwood and often finely carved. A ring of sheep bells consisted of ten or eleven; the smallest, a little tinkling bell, being number one, and two each of the other sizes.[21]

Life was lived very much on the English pattern among the country gentry of Toodyay and York; and nowhere could this be seen better than at Culham, the property of Samuel Pole Phillips — Squire Phillips, as he was usually called. The estate had its own little church, erected in 1853.[22] The homestead was large and comfortable, and its owner hospitable and genial, as a squire should be. He enjoyed a great reputation as a whip and a rider. He liked to drive a four-in-hand. The kangaroo hunts held at Culham were famous in the colony; his daughters, clad in black cloth habits and riding side-saddle, were foremost in the chase, and he liked one or other of them to accompany him each day when he rode about the estate. 'The best manure on the farm is the master's boot,' he used to say.[23]

Horse-breeding and racing were among his interests, and he owned a large cattle station further north on the Irwin River. He was as well known in Perth as he was in Toodyay. Governors and their ladies used to enjoy his hospitality; and there was nothing he liked better, if a warship were in, than to gather up a number of young officers and take them back to Culham for some hunting. It amused him to see their efforts to follow the fleet kangaroo dogs to the kill, when they were obviously more used to riding the waves.

The smaller farmers of Toodyay district had their own amusements. An account of the Newcastle Sports which took place in June 1872 lists:

> Cricket; jumping in sacks, bell in the ring, buns and treacle, grinning through a collar, hunting a pig with a greasy tail, wheeling wheel-barrows blind-folded, and foot-racing ... The whole wound up with a dance in the evening, no police interference being necessary throughout the day.

This triumphant statement points to the presence of many ticket-of-leave men in the community by that date. Quite a few ticket-of-leave holders had been enabled to settle on blocks of land made available to them by several philanthropic landowners of the district, such as James Drummond and J.H. Monger, who wished to encourage them in their return to free life. The opportunity existed, for such as would grasp it, to live down their past. Unfortunately, not many of them knew much about agriculture.

The pace of life over the hills was slow, and not particularly urgent, up to the seventies, as it was all over the colony. The convict poet O'Reilly caught the essence of it in some of his happiest phrases when he wrote:

> O beauteous Southland! Land of yellow air
> That hangeth o'er thee slumbering and doth hold
> The moveless foliages of thy valleys fair
> And wooded hills ...[24]

Then, as if a dream stirred a sleeper, or a strong wind blew from the east, several unrelated events occurred which served to wake up the isolated colony.

The seventies were the great days of Western Australian exploration. In 1869 a young member of the Survey Department named John Forrest had led a very small expedition consisting of himself, George Monger, Malcolm Hamersley, a farrier-blacksmith hired at Newcastle, and two natives to search for the remains of an earlier explorer, Leichhardt. Newcastle had been their jumping-off point, for some of their number came from there and the pack-horses were being procured there.[25] Not a great deal of interest was exhibited in this expedition, *The Inquirer* giving it only a short paragraph, for its readers had never heard of John Forrest. Five months later, on the party's return, *The Inquirer* printed Mr Forrest's journal, and reported that he had been entertained at a dinner given by twenty gentlemen.[26] Later, it remarked: 'We notice that a portion of the Melbourne press, while commenting on his expedition severely censures the poor and inadequate means placed at the disposal of exploring parties ...' It is pointed out that the camel, not the horse, is the animal specially fitted for the task of penetrating the unknown interior, and that there is no reason why horses should be longer employed, or in this instance why a number of camels should not be transferred from Victoria to the unexplored regions of the colony.[27]

Dr Mueller, the eminent Victorian botanist, whose idea it had originally been to search for the remains of Leichhardt, was very keen on the use of camels. Nevertheless, John Forrest managed his next, and more important expedition — overland to Adelaide — with horses. This time, on his return to Perth, he was accorded a much more enthusiastic account in *The Inquirer*, which now reported: 'A Complimentary Banquet to Mr Forrest, the Explorer, at the Horse and Groom Tavern, about seventy sitting down.'

John Forrest continued to put his faith in horses, and used them for his next expedition into the heart of the continent, in 1874. There were no camels to be had at this time in Western Australia, although as early as 14 January 1851, the *Government Gazette* had advertised that to any person importing one male and two female camels the Government would pay a bonus of £60, and £50 to the importer of two male and eight female alpacas. This offer had been repeated

154

again in 1858, but no one had claimed the bonus.

The strange beasts made their first appearance in Western Australia in 1875. At Culham some ten miles from Newcastle, one Saturday afternoon the ladies of the Phillips family were following the pursuits of any young lady of the time, when they suddenly heard a tremendous whinnying, a frenzied neighing, as all the horses on a property that devoted itself to the rearing of horses for the Indian market began carrying on as if the devil himself were at their heels. What they scented on the warm breeze they had never smelled before. The young ladies rushed out to the verandah of the long, low, shingle-roofed house, and saw, coming up the track from the road, a single file of odd-shaped beasts with a strange gait, ridden by men whose weather-beaten faces were as dark as Indians. But Indians they were not. It was the South Australian explorer, Ernest Giles, and his party, who had crossed the great Australian desert from Adelaide.

The party had touched Western Australian settlement farther north a few days earlier, had halted for several days' rest at Walebing, the home of Mr Lefroy, and on their way south had reached Culham on Saturday 13 November.

They remained several days at Culham. With gasps of delight, the young Phillips ladies were mounted on the camels and had their photographs taken. The youngest Phillips lady, aged ten, was entranced by the explorer himself, rather than the camels. 'Mr Giles was rather a small man. He had a hole in his nose and used to put a bone through it to amuse us children,' she was to recall, eighty years later.[28] On Sunday afternoon, a party from Perth arrived, headed by another small man — stocky, sturdy John

Forrest, fresh from his own triumphs — who had come to welcome Giles.

A message was sent in to the township of Newcastle so that its inhabitants could greet the Giles party on the morrow with appropriate celebrations. Newcastle was the first town to be reached in Western Australia.

With short notice, Newcastle did its best. The utmost enthusiasm prevailed. The whole district turned out. Near the bridge into the town, an arch was erected bearing the scroll, 'Welcome, Brave Explorer'. The Resident Magistrate and three Justices of the Peace met the party which arrived from Culham, and an address was read. Mr Giles thanked them briefly, for he was not a man of many words. The party was entertained to an excellent lunch at Ryan's Hotel, where sixty-five principal settlers met them. At the luncheon, a slight contretemps occurred after the champagne had flowed freely. The chairman, rising to propose the explorers' health, astonished them by remarking that he did not see why they had wanted to come over here, for there were 'plenty of our own'.[29] No doubt intended as a delicate compliment to John Forrest, it created quite a stir of protest, but it revealed the parochialism of some of the colonists: and whether they liked it or not, the east was coming more into touch with the west as the unknown interior lost its terrors and the desert was traversed.

The next morning the party started down the Newcastle road to Perth. 'It was a rare sight to see the camels marching in single file so docile and so biddeable,' says the newspaper account, following up with several funny stories of people who had never seen or heard of camels before.[30]

At Perth the welcome was even more enthusiastic. Two Volunteer companies lined each side of the route which was gaily decorated with bunting and streamers.

The time of entry was fixed for 3 o'clock, and punctual to the time Mr Giles and his party were espied crossing the bridge leading to the city. The explorers rode the faithful camels. They were dressed in bush costume, their rifles slung on to their pack-saddles, as in the wild interior their lives perchance often depended on these weapons. Altogether there were 18 camels, including an infant calf — ten of which acted as pack-camels carrying several 5 gallon kegs, strapped on the animals' backs. Mr Giles, who was accompanied by Mr Forrest on horseback, rode in front followed by other members of his party, Tommy the aboriginal lad, the best-dressed member of the expedition, bringing up the rear … Arriving at the Town Hall, the camels were with difficulty induced to take shelter in the market place, which forms the basement of the Hall, where they were locked in. On the party entering the Hall, the band struck up, 'See the Conquering Hero Comes …' A Banquet was held in the Town Hall on Saturday afternoon, with many toasts and much Champagne.[31]

Ernest Giles returned across the continent to Adelaide. In later years he entered the Western Australian Government service, died and was buried at Coolgardie, 13 November 1897. Forrest went on to further triumphs in political fields.

William Sykes, who may have stood among the crowd in Newcastle and gaped at the explorers and the camels, remained tied to his small and unimportant scope, which nevertheless was part of another phase of developing an expanding country.

When he arrived at Newcastle, Sykes would have had to report himself to the Resident Magistrate. The buildings of the former Convict Depot had been handed over to the police force in 1872 for living-quarters and offices. The large association ward for convicts had been converted into a Court House in front, and a schoolroom at the back, while the small convict hospital building with its cook-house, dead-house and closet remained for the purpose for which it was built.[32] Farther up the hill from the depot buildings a new lock-up, commenced in 1864, consisting of three cells, one native cell, kitchen and day-room; and quarters for a constable, had been built of the reddish-brown local iron-stone, with brick corners and shingled roof.[33] Its accommodation was later increased so that offenders convicted at Newcastle, Northam and Victoria Plains of lesser crimes could be imprisoned there instead of being sent to Perth under police escort, and could be used for local road-work. Its promotion from lock-up to gaol was declared in 1879.[34]

Sykes may have been attached to the Resident Magistrate as a general servant. The number of probation prisoners dispersed through the colony for 1875 shows that there were only two at Toodyay.[35] The Resident Magistrate states:

The prisoner at the Residency is generally employed for three or four hours a day in attendance to my house, cutting firewood, and keeping clean the dry earth closet; the rest of his time is spent within the walls of the prison.[36]

Early in 1876, Sykes must have received a letter — it would seem the first one — from his youngest child, William, writing instead of his mother, who had been ill, and giving his father, with a certain pride that he was able to do it, all the news of the family (Toodyay Letter No. 9). It is a wistful letter, to a father the boy could not remember at all, but of whom he had heard his mother speak so often. On Sykes's part, this family news from a son whom he vaguely recalled as a fair-headed baby must have seemed more and more unrelated to the kind of existence that he himself was living — as remote as the West Riding from the Toodyay valley. Almost forgotten, the work among the blazing furnaces of the Ironworks at Masbrough; constantly present, the slashing and grubbing of poison-weed, clearing and burning-off of scrub under a blazing bright, hard blue sky; for, although as soon as Sykes got his ticket of leave on 14 September 1877 he was hired to the medical officer, Dr Mayhew, as general servant, this easy work only lasted three months, and then he went on occasional work — grubbing, woodcutting out near the Moondyne Hills, fencing and labouring.[37]

Some time in 1876 he got the last letter that we know of from home. It has no date and is in a handwriting much inferior to any of the preceding letters, although stress of mind may account for this. It can only be dated approximately by previous references to the birth of Ann's children, and it incoherently expresses Myra's fears for the arrival of the third (Toodyay Letter No. 10). From now onwards, we hear Myra's voice no more, but this is not to say that she no longer wrote, or that anything had happened to her. It is more likely that the rest of her letters were lost at the time that the ones we know of were found, in 1931 (see Prologue). Myra herself lived on until 1894, and from what we know of her, it is unlikely that she ceased to write to her husband.[38]

Had he so wished, Sykes could have applied for his family to be sent out to Western Australia, once he had gained his ticket of leave. In the early days of the convict period the Government paid half the cost of passage of a family, but the rest had to be paid by the family itself, or the parish it came from, or by the ticket-of-leave man. This often was an obstacle to poor families, and after 1856 the method was abolished, and passage money for families was paid entirely by the British Treasury. In spite of this advantage, not a great many families were brought out. Many wives did not wish to leave England; and, on the other hand, many ticket-of-leave men did not apply for their families either because they had bigamously married again in the colony, or because they could not support them, or simply because they did not want them. It would seem that William Sykes was one of the last-named class.

After gaining his ticket of leave in September 1877, he apparently worked quite well in and around Toodyay until November 1879. From that time onwards for the next three years he was constantly drunk. 'Drunk and absent from place of abode, fined 10/-', 'Drunk, cautioned', 'Drunk in town, fined 5/-', 'Out after hours, fined 5/-', run the entries on his record.[39] Perhaps the realization of hopelessness had set in; small wonder if for him, and others like him, the waters of Lethe came only out of a bottle.

'Drunkenness is, as in former years, the prevailing crime,' runs the report of the Comptroller General in 1866.[40] He quotes it as being about 49.76 per cent of the whole of the offences recorded against free men, 55.98 of those against conditional pardon holders, and 41.78 of those recorded against ticket-of-leave holders. The percentages are not vastly different between bond and free. While heavy drinking was not generally regarded as a social evil, Governor Kennedy in 1856 had brought down on himself a great outcry on the part of the whole population by saying publicly that they all drank too much. He tried to improve the situation by bringing forward a Licensing Bill to correct laxity in the sale of liquor. A letter to *The Inquirer* on 16 July 1856 expressed the annoyance of the settlers that the Governor should think 'that the whole of the settlers are drunkards, and the use of ardent spirits has engendered a moral cancer, which it is his duty to remove ...' Governor Kennedy was not a temperance man — indeed, he was a connoisseur of old brandy, as the Reverend Archdeacon Wollaston bears witness;[41] he therefore saw with an unbiased eye the behaviour of the colonists, and the ticket-of-leave holders and the expirees. The chaplain at Fremantle gaol in 1854 was in a position to regard the conduct of convicts and re-convicted men. 'Many are tempted to seek a substitute for home and its happiness on the bench of the alehouse,' he reported in a picturesque phrase. He deplored that ticket-of-leave men had to struggle against a serious evil — the want of wives.

The clergy had always been in favour of having female convicts sent out in order to equalize the balance of numbers between the sexes.[42] It is likely that they were thinking more of the danger of rape than of drunkenness. Over the years, however, the incidence of rape and unnatural crime is extremely small. To quote only a few representative figures, in 1855 there was only one case of rape among 467 free men convicted of various crimes, and none from ticket-of-leave men convicted; while in 1866, rape and unnatural crime show one case each out of 1,217 crimes (see Appendix C).[43] Speaking in the Executive Council on the subject of bringing out female convicts, the Acting Comptroller General, Captain Wray, ascribed the infrequency of rapes and unnatural offences to the facility of cohabiting with native women. He was opposed to the idea of female convicts, and recommended pressing for more free female emigrants.[44] He was not alone in this; but reports of prison officials continue each year to refer to drunkenness being 'the fruitful and unfailing source of crime', proving that the prison chaplain was right in saying that consolation for lack of women was found among companions of the bar.

The British Government did its best to honour its promise to the colonists of Western Australia, on the formation of a penal settlement there, to send as many free emigrants as convicts. Between 27 July 1850 and 13 March 1855, ten emigrant ships arrived bearing 622 males, 1,032 females and 656 children.[45] The parliamentary vote for emigrants was stated to be expended on sending, first, the wives and families of well-conducted convicts; second, those of military pensioners going out as convict guards; third, females selected from union workhouses; and fourth, any balance that might remain, free emigrants selected under ordinary rules.[46] After 1855, there was a lag in emigrants owing to the labour market being unable to absorb them as well as ticket-of-leave men.

Obviously unmarried females were a necessity. A Census Return was taken on 30 September 1854, and again on 31 December 1859, the latter of which showed that thirty-eight per cent of adult males were married and sixty-two per cent single; while of females, seventy-two per cent were married and twenty-eight per cent single. The Census-takers reported:

> To this must be added the fact that of the men returned as married, 25 per cent. at least are virtually single, their wives residing in the United Kingdom, and of which but very few are likely to rejoin their husbands. This disproportion is daily increasing.[47]

By 1870, the total population of the colony was 24,785, of which 15,375 were males and 9,410 females.[48]

A number of young unmarried Irish girls had been among the free emigrants sent out between 1850 and 1855. They had been a good type of girl on the whole, and had married freely into the bond class. To this, and to their adherence to the moral principles of their Roman Catholic upbringing, one writer ascribes some of the success of the convict system.[49] Such marriages were an influence for good in the community, but there were all too few of them. In 1862, while the continuance of transportation was being considered, renewed efforts were made to send out free emigrants. A meeting in London of the National Association for the Promotion of Social Science approached the matter, and a Member of Parliament, dwelling on the necessity of sending out women, remarked that Irish girls were said to have no prejudice against marrying ticket-of-leave men. Another speaker, making the point that many convicts regarded transportation as a boon, rejoined in all seriousness: 'To go to a healthy climate, with an Irish girl, would be no punishment.'[50]

This lack of women had one important result. Sad as it was for the convicts, most of whom were reasonably young men when they received their freedom, they left few descendants. The convicts who did manage to marry usually made good and merged into the community. There must, however, have been many lonely men like William Sykes, who could see nothing ahead of them but death, who had no other companionship but that of their own kind, no cheer but what they found in drink.

At the time when the various convict depots were being closed, the *Perth Gazette* suggested that the untenanted buildings could be used for Bushmen's Clubs where men could gather, and where a good library could be provided. It remarked that alone of all the colonies, Western Australia was without a Bushmen's Club. 'Bushmen (in this colony mostly of the bond class), need such a club rather than the public house.'[51] The idea was good, but there was no one to follow it up. Free men and workmen had their clubs and Mechanics' Institutes scattered throughout the colony, but they were not keen on admitting expirees and ticket-of-leave men to them.

Among Sykes's letters as first found was an official form showing the sum deposited in the Savings Bank at Newcastle to the credit of William Sykes. On 26 September 1877, the amount was £10, probably denoting what Sykes had earned in gratuities during his probation working period. It had been one of Governor Hampton's innovations to establish a Savings Bank account for men going on ticket of leave so that they would not have the temptation to spend immediately on drink or bad companions a sum previously handed over in cash.

The following year Sykes withdrew the whole amount of £10, plus 5s. 7d. interest, on 31 July. He may have needed it for equipment, for shortly after this he was working at well-sinking with another man. December 1878 found him employed at Goomalling, some thirty-four miles from Newcastle, on the farm of James Ward. He evidently had some dispute with his employer, for among his letters is one from Ward dated 14 May 1897, acknowledging a rate of 5s. per foot for sinking a well (Toodyay Letter No. 11). Ticket-of-leave holders could complain to the Resident Magistrate when they thought the terms of agreement with employers had not been fulfilled. The fact that Sykes kept this letter shows that it had been needed. Well-sinking was work that paid well. The absence of permanent surface water made wells a necessity, and it was only in the late seventies that artificial reservoirs or dams began to be constructed.[52]

In taking up well-sinking, Sykes may have had the notion that somewhere, some time, he might strike gold. 'Yellow fever', as the local name for it was, had been a disease in the minds of men ever since the gold-rushes to the eastern colonies in the early fifties. Occasional signs of gold had been found in Western Australia and it seemed to everyone the desideratum even more needed than the convicts to set the colony on its feet. More elusive than a dream, it prompted the Government to advertise in the *Gazette* a reward of £5,000 for the discovery of a workable gold-field within a radius of 150 miles from the city of Perth. The noted New South Wales prospector, Mr E.H. Hargraves, offered to come and search various areas of Western Australia for gold, for a fee of £500 and expenses. The Government accepted his terms, but after making his examination he reported that the rocks of Western Australia were of a decidedly non-auriferous character.

Nevertheless, random traces of gold kept being found, and on 26 January 1869 the *Government Gazette* again advertised £5,000 reward for the discovery of a gold-field. This appeared weekly till April; later in the year, the radius of find was extended to 300 miles from Perth.

The following year, on 10 August 1870, *The Inquirer* headed a paragraph: 'Gold! Gold!! Gold!!!' It appeared that about May of that year small quantities of gold had been found in a gully below a hill named Peterwangy on the Upper Irwin River. Hopes of gold in payable quantities were immediately raised. Inspectors were sent to Peterwangy to make a report on the find; a nugget weighing about half a pennyweight was brought up, and many people left Perth and headed north.

'Within about 50 or 60 miles of the Gold Regions,' says one of them,

we had the good fortune to come up with a party of

166

four who were completely fitted out for a six months gold prospecting. They had a good team well loaded with every necessity and saddle horses to boot. All were armed cap-a-pie and presented a very resolute party.[53]

By September, about thirty people were camped on the ground, but many were dissatisfied and talked largely of giving the discoverer, George Brelsford, a thrashing for causing the stir. Only 'colour' was visible when earth was panned: no one discovered anything bigger than a peppercorn. By October *The Inquirer*'s special reporter wrote:

To prevent any more of the Perth people setting out for the reported gold fields, I address you a hasty line to let you know in what state we found matters. Peterwangy was totally deserted; there was no water and the ground as dry and hard as rock itself.[54]

The first Western Australian gold-rush was over. Nevertheless, continued news of gold came in from the northern regions. On 7 October 1874, *The Inquirer*'s correspondent from Victoria Plains reported:

The gold-seekers have just now forwarded to the city a team laden with quartz obtained a little to the north-west of New Norcia. It is to be hoped it will produce an alluring percentage of gold. The men are busily at work sinking through rock ...

Shows of the precious metal were found at Moondyne, Jimpeting (or Jumperdine) and Bailup, all within a radius of Newcastle. In spite of the Hargraves report, belief in the existence of gold somewhere in the colony was strong. Over ten years were to pass, however, before the second gold-rush, when payable gold was found much farther north, in the Kimberleys in 1885.

By that time, whatever dreams of wealth he may have harboured, William Sykes was beyond the hopes of gold. In 1883 he had been very ill for a month in Newcastle depot hospital, and left it in a debilitated state. He got his conditional release in 1885, and from then onward was virtually a free man, except that he was not allowed to proceed to the gold regions of the north. Before 1863, after a certain length of sentence had been served convicts were issued with conditional pardons, which permitted the bearer to leave the colony if he so desired. Opposition, partly from the eastern colonies, and partly from Western Australian settlers who saw their labour supply disappearing, caused the issue of conditional pardons to be replaced with conditional releases. The holder of a conditional release could not leave the colony till his full sentence had expired.[55]

Conditional releases were granted to men whose conduct had been uniformly good during the period of their ticket of leave. Apart from his bouts of drunkenness between 1879 and 1882, which never landed him in gaol, Sykes's conduct could have been termed good. He was evidently a very nondescript little man. There were people still living in Toodyay in the 1950s who could remember some of the later convicts, who

168

were distinctive in some way or another, but Sykes struck no chord in their memory.

The slow progression of the colony had been speeded up a little in one way by the exploring of its frontiers, and by the hopes of gold. In a more material way it was accelerated by the institution of telegraph lines between various centres in the early seventies and, towards the end of the decade, by the introduction of railways. In 1872 a railway from Perth to York and the eastern districts over the hills had been suggested, but it did not become an actuality till 1881, by which time it reached as far as Guildford. It took four more years to reach York. Meanwhile Toodyay was clamouring for the extension of the railway; the want of cheap and ready transport for produce from that centre was much felt. Not till 1887 did it get its extension of the York railway through a junction at Clackline.

William Sykes spent the last years of his life working on this line between Clackline and Newcastle, probably at maintenance work. It may have been at this time that he made the kangaroo-skin pouch for his letters, getting limp and tattered from much reading. He had a gun by this time, and now by the irony of fate could shoot as many of the animals of the wild as he liked. He had a dog, too, a good dog, perhaps a lean, slinking, gentle, yellow-eyed kangaroo-dog, to keep him company. It was a lonely life. Few settlers hade made their homes yet along the line, and the Newcastle road lay some miles west of it. Brilliant green parrots flashing through the bush, or magpies at dawn — 'Break-of-day birds', as they were called — or countless blowflies humming in the still heat of noon, supplied the only breaks in the silence; or a single crow flinging his harsh screech into the limitless, cloudless sky, than which there is no lonelier sound in the world. Sometimes the train would go rattling by, and newspapers would be tossed out to him, to pore over by lamplight, sitting at the rough table in his hut, sucking at his 'bush consoler', the little black-headed short pipe that most bushmen smoked. Sometimes a mounted policeman would call in, and be grumpily received.

Christmas Day of 1890 came in sizzling hot. A heat shimmer danced in the distance down the railway line. The line-maintenance man's hut was a little hell. It smelt of wood smoke, dry tea-leaves and bad meat. It was open to the dry wind like a breath from a furnace that coursed through it. The dog whimpered and moved from shade to moving shade. William Sykes, lying sick in his bunk, may have cast his mind back to that so different, snow-cold Christmas twenty-five years ago, when he entered upon the sentence that had brought him to this pass. His mates in the dock, the judge above, Myra in the gallery, Woodhouse — Woodhouse in the witness box, lying Sykes's life away: if he groaned, only the dog heard it.

Four days later, on 29 December 1890, the police at Newcastle received a report that William Sykes, conditional release holder, had been found ill and helpless in his hut on the Clackline railway. On visiting him, they had him removed at once to Newcastle hospital, at a cost of 3s. 9d. which they charged to the Inspector of Prisons, Perth.[56] He was just another old lag, a pauper to be Government-helped to death, one of many who were coming in from all over the colony at this time. If they still had a few more years' life left in them, they were sent down to Perth to the Mount Eliza Poorhouse, declared by the Resident Magistrate of from whatever district they came to be 'utterly destitute and unfit for work'. The routine phrase conjures up the worn-out bodies, now to be supported by the colony in which they had worked, even if unwillingly. If they were dying, and too ill to send to Perth, as was Sykes, there were still the hospitals of the former depots.

He lay in hospital five days. The doctor diagnosed his ailment as a hepatitic ulcer, with chronic hepatitis of about two months' duration. On 4 January 1891 he died.[57]

The Inspector of Prisons was informed that conditional release holder William Sykes, registered number 9589, aged sixty-three, had died; and duly noted the fact in red ink in the prison register, drawing a line to denote the end of that number's record. The Superintendent of Poor Relief was notified that number 9589 William Sykes had been provided with a coffin by the Government, which would have to be replaced. The cost was £2 15s. 0d. 'There is a sum of £1-4-10, proceeds of a sale of a dog belonging to the deceased in the hands of the police,' the Resident Magistrate went on. 'Shall I forward the amount to you or to the Curator of Intestate Estates? There are also a few effects of the deceased in the hands of the police, of but trifling value and will hardly sell.'[58]

Among these effects of 'trifling value' must have been the kangaroo-skin pouch containing William Sykes's letters. Piled up with a few old clothes and a battered gun, it lay on a shelf in the police office. Nine months later, the police managed to sell the gun for £1, which they forwarded to the Inspector of Prisons.[59] They may have despaired of selling the other effects and perhaps gave the old clothes to natives. Some disturbance of the effects evidently took place, in the course of which the

171

fur pouch dropped down into a crevice behind the shelves, and lay there undiscovered for thirty years.

The police office to which Sykes's things had been taken was at the end of a row of buildings beyond the hospital and Court House. These buildings had been the warders' quarters of the old Convict Depot. In 1872, when the depot buildings were handed over to the Colonial Government, the warders' quarters became quarters for the sergeant of police.[60] Later this office, partitioned into three cells and a day-room, became a gaol for females, and a room at the end of the police quarters had to be yielded up for an office. As the years went on, this office became too small. New police quarters were built in 1920 in Duke Street, which bounded the former convict grant.[61] The old buildings, disused, became dilapidated and unsightly, and the Toodyay Road Board decided to approach the authorities about having them pulled down. On 27 August 1931, the *Toodyay Herald* reported that the Public Works Department had given the Road Board permission to demolish the buildings. When the demolition took place, all the accumulated papers left behind as unwanted at the time of the move to new quarters in 1920 were scattered to the winds. As the walls were pulled down, and fittings and woodwork came away, out fell the kangaroo-skin pouch and by mere chance was picked up by someone who had the sense to hand it on to a member of the Historical Society. There, as has been shown, it once again escaped destruction.[62]

It remains now to judge whether the Toodyay letters were worth preserving. The poor have no heirlooms of gold or silver to leave behind them when they die. William Sykes left a dog and a gun that nearly paid for his burial; and, more enduring, he left a bundle of tattered letters that tell of a woman's steadfast and unchanging love for a convict. Not much, perhaps; and yet, too much to be utterly forgotten.

There is little that can be said in extenuation of William Sykes. He killed, or helped to kill, another man. His story is the story of many convicts of the period who were sent to Western Australia. They came, they worked, they died. If they left any traces on the national character, as it was feared they would, these might be said to be, perhaps, a dislike for authority, a toughness, and a kind of rough fairness as expressed in the common phrase, 'give a man a go'. Such traces, or other perceptible ones, are no grounds for shame. The convicts came at a time when they were badly needed. They, and the expenditure that supported the system, held a disintegrating colony together for the length of time necessary for it to become a whole. Bonded into the structure of its history like the chequered bricks of the buildings they erected, they cannot be disclaimed.

The later convict period undoubtedly had reformatory aspects that were lacking in the earlier and harsher years in other colonies. As shown by despatches, and by books of the period on the punishment and prevention of crime, the national conscience of the country transporting convicts had been aroused; and within the scope of their times, convicts were treated as human beings who had taken a step on the wrong path. In sending them to a new country it was stressed that there they could make good, have a fresh chance, be removed from their environment. They may not have believed it; but the chance was there, and remained for those who believed to take it. A considerable number of convicts in

Western Australia did, in fact, make good, acquire property, marry and melt into the community. The fact that after the influx of convicts there was not a great deal of added crime in the community shows either that the impulse, or the incentive, was not there; and the fact that no system of assignment of convicts to settlers was allowed meant that the conditions amounting almost to slavery which had pertained in the early years of New South Wales and Van Diemen's Land were never present in Western Australia. Ticket-of-leave and conditional release men were paid at the current rate of labour and could appeal to Resident Magistrates if they objected to conditions of pay or work.

There was, at first, as shown by diaries and accounts of the seventies, a social barrier between bond, or ex-bond, and free, which was overcome in the next generation or two. By that time, if older people could still nod towards certain persons and say wisely, 'Ah, *he* didn't choose to come out here,' or, 'That one didn't pay his own passage,' younger people were not interested enough to remember who they were. By that time too, many convicts had died without issue, and many expirees had left the colony. A Register of Expirees and Conditional Pardon Holders who have left the Colony: Port of Albany shows that in thirty years, between 7 January 1863 and 6 May 1893, 801 ex-convicts departed from the colony and of these, only forty-seven returned. Albany was the most general port of departure because steamships put in there instead of at Fremantle.

As regards population, the convicts did not make very great additions to the numbers. In the eighteen years during which transportation took place, only 9,669 convicts arrived, many of whom departed when their sentences had been served. The gold-rushes brought more population in a brief time than did transportation, the first real 'rush' in 1886 bringing 5,615 arrivals to the colony in that year; and the 'rushes' of 1894 and 1895 bringing 25,858 and 29,523 arrivals respectively.[63] Like the convicts, many of these did not remain. Since population figures include natural increase, and it has been pointed out that the convicts did not have much influence on this, for lack of mates, it may be concluded that the gold-rushes, which brought females as well as males to the colony, had a greater effect on the population.

It must also be remembered that in the colony of Western Australia there was always the backbone of good settler society — old soldiers of many wars, Peninsular and Waterloo veterans; old sailors who had seen service on the Seven Seas. At a later date, contemporary with the convicts, came the military pensioners and their families, men who had fought at Alma and Inkerman and Sebastopol, and in the Indian Mutiny. These two classes of people were strongly in evidence in the seventies and even in the nineties. A journalist of the time, Gilbert Parker, visiting Western Australia in 1891, found not mainly a convict society but:

> more gentlemen of the very old school than in any place in Australia ... You will be met with the invitation to take a pinch of snuff from a gold snuffbox; you will come into an area of oldtime after-dinner conversation; you will imagine yourself sometimes in the days of William IV or of the First Gentleman in Europe.[64]

This may mean that Western Australia was behind the times, or that, although a great many of the first generation of colonists had died, their sons were framed in the same mould, and determined the sort of society imposed at the top level. They also, as much and more than the convicts, had their share in determining a national character.

The more material traces of the convicts are fast vanishing. Many of the roads they made have been re-surveyed and bull-dozed out of new country. A few buildings whose purpose has been forgotten and whose walls are crumbling remain in country towns. Other quite handsome buildings in Perth and Fremantle, whose design recalls the Old World from which their architects came, are marked for destruction by the hand of progress. Soon the convicts will have no monuments.

William Sykes has no monument. He was buried in a nameless grave in the cemetery of Toodyay, at the back of the Protestant section, outside the consecrated ground, in a part reserved for convicts, paupers and suicides, on the slope of a hill covered in summer with dry yellow grass.[65] Two funeral cypresses and a yew shed a strong sweet scent on the hot summer wind, and William Sykes is in good company at last, for below him on the hill lie other bones that once were stout settlers, their lives given, like his, to their new country.

*The Toodyay Letters*

The Toodyay Letters are reproduced exactly, line for line, as they were written. Each block of text within each letter represents a separate page of the original.

# [1]

15 March 1867
Dear husband i rite these
few line to you hopeing
to find you better than it
leaves us at present i have
been very uneasy sinse you did
not rite my children cried
When we got no leter Mrs Bone
has got two leters sinse i got
one will you please to rite to
me and send me wird how
you are getting on i have bilt
myself up thinking i shall get

to you some time or another
My mother sends her best love
to you she has been very ill
but she is better at present
we all send hour kind love
to you we all regret very much
for you i hope their will be a
lighting for you yet Woodhouse
has been giving hiself up
severl times when he has been
in drink i hope he will your
John and Emma send their
love to you we have wished scores

of time you were comeing in to the
house we should syuse you to deth
for we could like to see that
Jhon ward lives next door to
us he sends his respects to you
his Wife his pius womman

she talks about you very
often Joshua Sykes has sent
word for me to go to their
house but i have not had
time to go you must not delay
riteing if you can it will ease
my mind if you can

if ever it lays in your power
to send for us when you get
abroad i would freely sell
all up to come to you if i
possibly could for health
  Dear farther do pleas
to writ to is i Sends one 100
kiss for you thirza Sykes
            a kiss will xxxxx
Anrr Sykes sends Dear xxxxx
father i send a 100 kiss for you
Alfredd sens kiss kinds
Love to you     Masbro
Midland Road 33

[2]

Masbro' 19 March 1867
My dear Husband —
I have this afternoon received
your letter and am glad
to hear from you — I heard yesterday
that there was a letter from
you at Park-gate and wrote off
immediately to the Governor of
the Portsmouth prison asking
him to kindly send me word
if he could what was the
latest day I could see you, as
I do not see how I could pos
sibly undertake the journey
this week, being without mo
ney, If I had received your

letter on Saturday, it was
the reconing and I would have
done my best to contrive it –
But if you do not leave before
the next reconing I will come if
I come alone for none of them
say anuthing about coming themselves, or assisting me to do so either
so far. I feel it as much as you do
to be very hard for you to be

where you are and Woodhouse
at liberty, but rest assured
whether I git to see you or not I
hope that when you arrive at
your journeys end you will not
forget us, for we are always thinking
about you. I hope the
governor will either send me a
reply or allow you to do so, for I
will leave no means untried to
get to see you if there is time
but if I was at the expense only
to be too late when I got there
it will be a serious loss to me
situated as I am. I feel greatly
hurt that you should send your
letters to you Brothers & Sisters
before me — for although we are
separated there is no one I value
and regard equal to you — and
I should like you to still have
the same feeling towards me,

and if there is ever a chance
of our being permitted to join
you again even though it be
in a far off land, both the
children and myself will most

gladly do so — Mr Bone has
written to his wife to get the
childrens likenesses taken for him

to take away with him I should
like you to have ours if you
are allowed the same privilege
Will you let me know? I cannot
give you up. I live in the hope of
our being together again somewhere
before we end our days — My best
love to you, the children also send
their love to you, and love and
remembrance from all friends
your affectionate wife — Myra Sykes

## [3]

This is intended for William Sykes number 283
Portsmouth Prison

Sir

Governor of this prison Sir it is not my wish or will to go against
the rules or Regulations of this prison and I hope and trust
through your instrumentality that William Sykes Convict
number 283 will receive this into his hands and i hope
it will not miss his heart and i wish to inform him
that his wife and children Brothers and Sisters are
all well at present for ought i know we send our dearst
and kindest respects to you hopeing it will find you in
good health, William my advice to you is that you
obey all that are in authority over you and Let
your conduct be good and try to gain that which
you have lost i mean your character Let me beg of you
to pray to our heavenly father and his son
Jesus Christ to give you a clean heart and right sprit
within and then all your troubles and anxieties of this
world will be small when compared with the
Joy and happyness of that bright world above William
I hope you are aware that our Blessed Lord has
Caused all holy scriptures to be written for our
learning and God Grant that we may hear and
read them and not to read them only but to do what
they teach us and then when the swelling of Jordan overtakes

us may we be ready to meet our saviour and him be ready
to convey us through the valley and shadow of death to our
heavenly father arms there everlasting to dwell with him Dear
Brother i ask you to seek for Christian salvation which

means deliverance from something that is feared or suffered
and it is therefore a term of very general application, but in
reference to our spiritual condition it means deliverance from
those evils with which we are afflicted in consequence of our
departure from God it implies deliverance from ignorance
from ignorance of God, the first and the last the greatest
and the wisest, the holiest and the best of beings, the maker
of all things, the centre of all perfection, the fountain of
all happiness, ignorant of God we cannot give him
acceptable worship we cannot rightly obey his will
we cannot hold communion with him here we cannot be
prepared for the enjoyment of his presence hereafter
But from this ignorance we are rescued by the salvation of the
Gospel, which reveals God to us which makes us acquainted
with his nature, his attributes his character, his government
and which especially unfolds to us that scheme of mercy
in which he has most clearly manifested his glory
it is good that a man should both hope and quietly wate
for the salvation of the Lord. William a few more words
when they was leading Jesus to the cross and there followed
a great company of people who also bewailed and lamented
him but Jesus turning unto them said Daughters of
Jerusalem weep not for me but weep for yourselves

Well William in conclusion i will say a little about
the contents of your letter, i believe you said your children
was the strings of your heart now i say let Christ be
the strings of your heart i believe you went on to say that
wentworth was your place of birth and i say let
Christ be your salvation

William your brother John sends his best
respects to you hopeing the advice Given will have
a good effect your sister Rebecca sends her love
to you and trusts she will see you again before
death do you part and your sister Elizabeth sends
her kindest love to you wish you to behave yourself
under your present situation and as for me C
Charles Hargreaves my desire is to point
you to the Lamb of God that takes away the sins of the
world and trust in Christ as your Physician
for it is through him we Live and move and
have our being Dear William your brother John
would give your little boy a good school education
but your Dear Wife cannot find time to send
him to school i conclude with the blessing of God
almighty the father the son and the holy Ghost
may remain with you both now and for ever amen i trust
the governor of this Prison is a kindhearted
Man   Charles Hargreaves Park Gate near Rotherham
Yorkshire.

**[4]**

Masbro' 8 April 1867
My dear Husband —
I have this day sent off a
box for you which I hope you
will receive safely — I have
sent you all that I possibly
could and am only sorry
that it is not in my power
to send you more — as soon
as I received your letter I took
it to Elizabeth — She has
sent you two of the smallest
spice loaves, and gave me 1s
towards the expenses — Then I
went to Rebecca and she
could not do anything towards

it. Emma has sent the other
spice loaf and mince pie — &
Elizabeth the testament and
tract, and John the other two
books, and the remainder I
I have sent myself — I hope
you will write back the very
first opportunity to let me
know if you have received
it. I have paid 4/6 carriage

to Bristol they will send us
word what it costs from there
to the ship, and John will
pay that, I should like you
to write as often as ever you
can, and when you write next
send word whether a few post
age stamps will be of any
use to you — I walked to Shef
field yesterday morning in the
hope of getting a good shut
knife for you, but could
not meet with any of them
Sailor Bill is very well but
I did not see him, and Chas
Salt has gone into the North
and Edw. Uttley sends his best
respects to you. If Saturday
had been pay day I might
perhaps have been able to get
a trifle more for you I called

at John Cliffs they sent their
love to you & Mrs sent an ounce
of Tobacco — We also send our best
love to you and the children all
wish they were going in the
same ship with their Father. I
have enclosed you a list of the
articles in the box and M ....

encloses a packet of needles
with his respects — If you have
the chance to earn any money in
Australia you must save it all up
and I will do the same, that
if there is a chance of our rejoin
ing you we may be able to do so.

Be sure to write and let me know if
you have recd the box for I shall not
be easy in my mind until I hear from
you again — Remaining with best
love and wishes for your welfare.
Your affectionate wife — Myra Sykes.

## [5]

Masbrough    20 September 1868
Dear Husband I take this oportune
-ty of writing you these few lines
to you to let you know that
I receved your letter datee the
July the fifth 1868 Dear
Husband I was glad to heir
that you were well and in good

(bottom of page torn)

whither I had got one from you
or not and that put me about for
I thought that something had
happened to you because their
was no letters for me and I was
much further put about when I
receved your letter when it was a
week amongst them before I got it
Dear husband when you write again
send me word what sort of a pashege
you had when you were going out
and send word whither you got that
box that I sent you when you
were leving this country for you
never said in your letter whither you
got it or not I am very sorry to be

(page missing)

Old house still and they all

send their kind love to you and
Edward Huttley and his wife
sends their kind love also and your
daughter Ann is in place and doing
well and Alfread is working in the
    –al mill and he gets10 pence per day
Ann Thurza Alf William sends their
kind love to you but William has
got long white curly hair and he

was not called William for nothing
for he is a little rip right and your
Brothers and sisters sends their kind
love to you and their was another

(page torn)

This took place on Lord
Warncliffs Eastart the Keepper
was Shot.
               Berdshaws Father
took it so much to heart that he went
and through himself on the rails
and the trains past over him and
Kiled him

191

Dear Husband
when you write again Derect
your letter to Mrs Sykes No 39
Midland Road Masbrough

# [6]

Greasbrough    4 Nov 1869
Dear Husband I take this
opertunety of writing you
these few lines to let you
know that me and all the
Children are all well hoping
that when you receve this
letter you will be in good
helgth as this leves us all at present
thank God for his kindness to
us all Dear Husband it has
been three weeks since I hard
that their was a letter came to
your Sister and I did went to
the post office to see whether it
was right or not and I found out
that their had been one but I
have never seen it yet and Ann
had seen whether hir Ant Bacer
would not let hir see the letter but

She said that she would not
let me nor hir see the letter so
the children has taken it greatly
to heart and they are never done
speaking about it and they never
gave me any pease since but I

have been waiting with the greates
of pacientes till they had all
seen your letter that I might
know how to write to you but
they will not give it up
so the children would have
Me write to you without
Seeing your letter but Ann
is the worst of them all about
it and She is bothered greatly
About it every day in hir life
about it wheir she is serving
for all your old friends in
Gresbrough they are wanting to

know how you are geting
on their is some of your old
friends in the house where she
is every night in the week that
is in Harriss But Dear Husband
I cannot tell what they have
all got against me for I have
never yet bothered them for
nothing since you left us all
But Dear Husband I have work
ed hur for my Children and
myself Since you went
I have done my uttermost

to bring them up as well as
any other persons Children
about the place and I have
done so yet thank God

We are living in Gresbrough
and Alf is in the pit working
and Ann is place and Thurza
and William is going to the
School and by the time I
get a letter from you I hope
Thiza will be able to write
to you Dear Husband my
brother Alfred is always bad
the same as my Brother Manuel
was before he died and he
sends his kind love to you and
all our familey does the same
Ho and I had my Brother
Ellis and his son Lodging with
me for some time but they
went back to Bannesley
the work was slack there but
it is much better now

# [7]

9 March
Dear Husban I been long
In writing to you I hope you will
forgive I receved you letter
and was plesed with it I think
you mite send me more word
wot your doing I hope this will
find you in good health as
it leves us at present I want you
to send a lineto Alfred
he is geting up likes to go
to the public But is not a
Bad lad to me and I expect
you will be a grandfather of to
Wenn this Letter arrive at you
Ann on Again she not very
good Luck lost a dule of time
from binn poly but he
Lucking well my littel Bill as
as been very poly he is
Better and Looks well

I want to now if you Write
to your Brother Jos i have seen
him ons I think cince you
went away I hearit say that
if Mr Mondeller git in the

elictions for Sheffield that
he wood be abel to have some
convesation with him and
try to do something for you
it harte Bricks me to write
like this if the prodigal son
cud come Buck to his home
wons more thare woold be
a rejoicing I must tel you
that my brother Herbit as
as got very bad Brunt I
expecte as been getting Drunk
linge on the flor I have not
been to see him I must tell
you that Mr Mondeller got
in for Sheffield and I hope he
will do you good

and you mencend about
Lucking yong I thort you
did when I saw you at Leeds
my hart Broke neley wenn I
felt your hand bing so soft.
Dear Husban you wood be seprice
to see Wot a grit fine lucking
girl Tirza is it will be my
Birth day on Tuensday 17 of March
as for my self I not lucking
very well at present
Brother and sister sends there

best love to you John tell
friends often ask if i ever
hear of John thay not yet
Alfred is in the Woinbel main
pit and Ann Husban and my
Brother Ellis Alfred full
week 19 6 pence he minden
genger

Ann Husban says He
Wood Work Hard for you
to come hom if it cud
be Done and my
and my Dear Husban
I sends my nearest
and Dearest Love to you
and all the children
with A 1000 Loves and
kiss wish We may meet
again ho that We
cold in this World

## [8]

11 April 1875
Dear Husband I writ
these few lines to you
hoping to find you well
as it leaves us at present
we receved your letter dated
12th of January and was
glad to recieved it and we
recived your letters you directed
to kit royal I dont douted but
you have rote a many letters
that I never heard tell of I
wonce was thee years and
had not had a letter ... your
relations said that you was
Dead I went to Rotherham
townshall and asked if they
knew wheather you was dead
or not one of the police sade
he heard you was desd

I put the chealdren
and my self in black
for you my little Tirza went to
the first place in deap Black
then I heard that your sister
Elizabeth had got a letter

from you my daughter Ann
went to see if they had told her
that you was all rite and
and they told her that ther
letter had gone to Sheffild
she could not see it that wan
the time you wass directed them
to your sister Dear Husband
Elizabeth fected the Bible
and Robinson crewsaw
while I was at the Leeds asices
I bleve John has them
John is living at the
barrow in farnsess in Yorth

I donth now drections
I lent Rebacca five shiling
to go to Leeds with and never
gave that back I had to do
the best way I coud for my
cheldren and my self
Dear Husband cant express
myself to you but I hoap to see
you wonse more seeted in
corner I will the beest for
you if it coms to pass
Some days I feel pretty
cheerful and others very sad
sad But I think it is
owing my age well I

must tell you that Ann geting
Again for A nother and
am sorry to tel you that
he is not one of the best
of Husban

Dear Husban I must tell
my Alfred I beleve is
toler than you pepel is
seprsed with him
Thirza I belive she not
far off 11 stone william
nist boy he does not luse
a inch of is ight but Ann she
would be cross with me if
new I sent you wird

I don't think he is veary
fond of work he is a unculted
man peter Looffield
very best respect to you he doing
well he Loves that house that Tamer
selars ned Utley sends Love to you
My brothers and Sister best Love –
xxxxx xxxxx Luke Booth send is
respects he lives at the wite
house ould Mr Crssland

## [9]

20 October 1875
Dear father I write these few lines
hopeing to find you better than it
leaves us at present my mother as
been very ill and me my self
and I am a bit better Dear father
we think you have quite forgot us all
my sister Ann takes it hard at
you not writing oftener I must
tel you that sister Ann as to nice
boys the oldest is a fine little
fellow well I must tell you what
a stout young man my brother
Alfred as got and Thirza is a
stout young woman poor Ann
is very thin Ann usband and
Alfred works at aldwarke

Main pit Edward Uttley sends his
kindest love to you he as a large
famuley they have nine children
uncles and hants sends there kindest
love to you we dont live far
from hand rebacco france I
often play with there little boy
my hant often say I am like
my father there oldest boy

William as been dead fifteen mounths
my uncle John as been over from
barring furnace and he looked very well
very well Dear father you woul
Would hardly know Greasbrough
now if you seed it we have got
a new congregational church and I go
to that school
Dear father Mother would
like to no if they would alow
you our likeness Dear father
you never name me in you
letters but I can sit down and
write a letter to you now

Dear father my mother wants
to now if you ever hear of
been sat free we all send
kindest and dearest love to
you and God bless you
and 1,000 kisses for our Dear
father from your Dear
son William

# [10]

Dear Husban I am grvd
to my hart A bout my
Ann I have had her
Both times of her
confindments and
Ly shee gating on
gain
We hall sends out
nearst and dearst
                    Love to you
with A 1000 kiss
Dear Husband you
must excuse writing

## [11]

14 May 1879                    To Well Sinkers
                        in care of Mr C. Adams
William Sykes –
    When I went to New-
castle I looked at
the Agreement and
I find you and your
mate were right in
what you said 5
shilling foot for every
five feet I did not
beleive that I made
that bargain with yous
but I see now that
I did.          W.T.


I am quite willing to settle
to settle with you when
I here from either of yous
yous plase send
word      your James Ward

*Appendices*

# Appendix A

*Resolutions of a Meeting Held to Determine Whether Western Australia Should Apply to Become a Penal Settlement*

AT a public meeting held at the Court House, Perth, Western Australia, on Friday, 23 February 1849, G.F. Stone Esq., High Sheriff, in the chair, the following Resolutions were proposed and carried:

*1st*. Resolved, that this colony is at present in a state of great depression, caused by the exhaustion of the important elements of capital and labour.

*2nd*. Resolved, that the whole capital of the settlers being already invested, and that too in pursuits which yield no profitable return, the means of the colony are inadequate to the promotion and completion of the various schemes of improvement which the still undeveloped resources of the country suggest, and which would be highly impracticable under more favourable circumstances, while the difficulty is still further increased by the steady and constant emigration of labour from the colony.

*3rd*. Resolved, that the meeting can see no remedy for such a position other than one which shall have the effect of speedily introducing fresh capital to supply the place of that which has been lost, and new and abundant labour to meet the drain that has taken place in the old.

*4th*. Resolved, that this meeting views with great regret and alarm the introduction by the Home Government of persons drafted from the various penitential asylums in England, and men on tickets of leave, as being a course quite unsuited to the wants of the settlers, and as tending to make matters worse instead of better. That this course, at the very best, would meet only half the evil, viz., the insufficient amount of labour without providing at all for the other and more important half — the want of capital. Labour without the means of employing it being a burthen rather than a benefit, while the introduction of persons of this class without any precaution being taken or fund created for the establishment of an adequate guard, either of police or military, to protect the colonists, would of itself be an evil of very great magnitude, the colonial revenue being totally insufficient to meet any part of this necessary expense.

*5th*. Resolved, that this meeting, believing that some great change is necessary to the welfare, and even to the existence of this colony, and bearing in mind also the evident intention of the Home Government to make it indirectly the receptacle of convicts by pouring in upon us felons under the various names of 'exiles', 'probationers' and the like, thereby inflicting upon us all the evils of a convict colony, without the necessary protection and expenditure, considers it advisable, under the circumstances, that application should at once be made to Her Majesty's Government, to erect this colony into a regular penal settlement, with the necessary Government establishment and expenditure, the whole cost of the transmission, maintenance, and supervision of all such convicts as may be transported hither being borne, of course, by the Home Government.

*6th*. Resolved, that the establishment of a penal settlement in this colony would seem to present some advantages to the Home Government to counterbalance the expense of the measure, inasmuch as the convicts would be employed in developing profitable resources which at present are totally useless, either to the mother country or to the colony, from the want of adequate means in the settlers to render them available. Of these may be enumerated the promising mines of lead and coal recently discovered to the northward and southward, and the exhaustless supply of fine timber, an article of especial value to the mother country, and which could serve to freight home the ships by which the convicts are conveyed.

*7th.* Resolved, that a full representation of the objects of this meeting shall be made to His Excellency the Governor, and that for this purpose a deputation from this meeting, to consist of Messrs W. Burges, A.O.G. Lefroy, Thomas Helms, Robert Habgood, and G. Shenton, with power to add to their numbers, be appointed to wait upon His Excellency with a copy of the resolutions passed, to solicit the assistance of the local government in carrying out the purposes of this meeting, and to request His Excellency to take all such proper steps as may be necessary to put Her Majesty's Secretary of State for the Colonies in full possession of the facts of the case; and that the gentlemen forming such deputation shall also be a permanent committee for the purpose of organizing the scheme and of communicating generally with the local government and others on the subject.

(Parliamentary Papers on Convict Discipline and Transportation, vol. VI, Governor Fitzgerald to Earl Grey, 3 March 1849, Enclosure)

# *Appendix B*

## The Nature of the Convicts Sent to Western Australia between 1850 and 1868

A tradition has grown up in Western Australia that the convicts sent there when the colony was a penal settlement were of a different nature from those sent to the earlier penal colonies of Australia. They are popularly supposed to have been 'good' convicts, guilty only of minor offences, who did not in any way lower the moral tone of the colony that 'consented' to receive them. Since this conception must have its origin somewhere, let us examine the sources from which it might have come, and whether it was true.

The convict period of Western Australia's history has been much neglected, only two works having been devoted to it in this century, and neither of them so far published. The more comprehensive of the two is: 'The Convict System in Western Australia, 1850–1870', by C. Gertzel; the second, mainly concerning a notable Fenian prisoner, is 'Behind the Lighthouse: A Study of the Australian Sojourn of John Boyle O'Reilly', by Martin C. Carroll, Jr. The first-named is a thesis written for the Honours Degree in History of the University of Western Australia, 1949; the other is a Dissertation submitted in Partial Fulfilment of the Requirements for the Degree of Doctor of Philosophy in the Department of

English at the State University of Iowa, USA, 1954.

In *Western Australia: A History from its Discovery to the Inauguration of the Commonwealth*, by Dr J.S. Battye (Oxford University Press, London, 1924), portions of three chapters and an appendix deal with the convict period; and in an earlier *History of West Australia*, by W.B. Kimberly (F.W. Niven and Co., Melbourne, 1897), three chapters treat the convict period with a good deal of detail; while *A Story of a Hundred Years*, edited by Sir Hal Colebatch (Perth, 1929), a volume brought out to mark the centenary of the State, manages to tell the story without alluding to the convicts at all.

The most recent of the works mentioned above — 'Behind the Lighthouse' — states on page 112:

> When transportation began it was stipulated that no hardened criminals would be sent out but rather able-bodied and well-conducted men, not over 45 years of age, who still had at least half their sentences to serve, and none of whose sentences were less than 7 years.

Carroll gives as his references: Battye, page 459, and Gertzel, page 4.

On turning to the page in Battye's Appendix on the Convict System to which Carroll refers, the relevant passage reads:

> In accordance with the agreement made by the Home authorities with the colonists, the men sent out were to be able-bodied, not over forty-five years of age, well conducted in prison, and having at least half their sentences to run, such sentences on conviction having been for not less than seven years. It was also stipulated on the part of the colonists — who must have been very

212

innocent if they thought the stipulation would ever be observed — that no criminals of a reckless or dangerous class should be sent out. Convicts from Irish jails were not to be transported, nor were female offenders. This last condition was strictly carried out ...

This Appendix has no numbered references, but has at the end a list of works consulted, among which is: *The British Convict in Western Australia* (London, 1865), by H. Willoughby (a journalist attached to the Melbourne *Argus*). This book is given by Gertzel as her reference when using much the same terms as in the two passages above to describe the sort of convicts transported to Western Australia.

Willoughby, on page 31, says:

In accordance with the agreement made with the colony, the men sent out should be able-bodied, not over 45 years of age, well-conducted in prison, under sentence to not less than seven years' confinement, and having more than half of this term to run. It was also agreed — the circumstance is ludicrous, but no less true — that a reckless and dangerous class should not be sent out. England, in short, was to send out the men she could manage herself, and keep those she could not. I heard convict officials allude to this agreement as 'moonshine' and it is well known that, in one instance at least, instructions were given to the English subordinates to ship all the desperadoes they could pick out. The rule, if ever observed, is now abrogated. Governor Hampton has expressed his readiness to accept ordinary convicts, and the form of moral selection is now dispensed with. Neither female convicts nor convicts from the Irish gaols have ever been sent out.

From the wording of the above paragraph, used by Battye, Gertzel and Carroll, Willoughby therefore appears to be the primary source for the description of the men sent out as convicts. It would seem that he had doubts himself as to the likelihood of some of his information. The manner in which he obtained it will be dealt with later. Was it, in fact, correct?

He uses such terms as 'agreement' with the colony and, 'it was agreed' (changed to 'stipulated' by Battye) which imply that conditions were made by the colony and accepted by the British Government previous to the actual sending out of the convicts. Such was not the case. The Minutes of the Executive Council of Western Australia make no mention of any 'agreement' although they detail the steps taken to secure the formation of a penal settlement.

As the culmination of four years of agitating for convicts by certain sections of the community of Western Australia, a public meeting was held in the Court House, Perth, on 23 February 1849, and a series of resolutions was proposed and carried, setting out the depressed state of the colony and appointing a deputation to wait upon the Governor, Captain Charles Fitzgerald, to make known to him the feeling of the meeting, and to request him to petition her Majesty's Secretary of State for the Colonies to make Western Australia a full penal settlement with all the expenses thereof to be borne by the Home Government. At no point in these resolutions does it occur that any conditions as to the sort of convicts were suggested; nor in accounts of the meeting contained in the two newspapers, the *Perth Gazette* and *The Inquirer*, is there any sign that conditions were even thought of. All that the settlers wanted was convicts — any sort of convicts — as long as there were enough of them, and the expense of their maintenance and supervision was borne by the British Government.

As this suited the plans of the British Government, Earl Grey, Secretary of State for the Colonies, sent a despatch to Governor Fitzgerald acquainting him that free emigrants would be sent out in numbers equal to the male convicts received by the colony. (P.P., vol. IV, Grey to Fitzgerald, 12/7/1849) The intentions of the Government were further signified in a letter from the Under-Secretary for the Colonies, Benjamin Hawes, reiterating the Government's intention to send an equal number of free settlers, and asserting that there would be no system of assignment of convicts to settlers. Mr Hawes stated that a moderate number of convicts to be used on public works would be sent out, the whole expense defrayed by the British Treasury. They would be selected for good conduct, and from having no long period to serve before their tickets of leave were due. Earl Grey himself pointed out that the selection of men of good conduct was a necessity at this period, as there was no gaol ready for their safe keeping; but no statement was made that good conduct would *continue* to be a principle of selection. (*Colonial Policy of the Administration of Lord John Russell*, by Earl Grey, vol. II, p. 58)

These were the only promises made by the British Government to the colonists before the arrival of the convicts; and they were announced, not agreed upon. Indeed, there is evidence to suggest that the colonists were disappointed with the sending out of a few convicts selected for good conduct, soon to be free on tickets of leave. The Comptroller General of Convicts pointed out in July 1850 that there seemed to be a misconception among the settlers as to the kind of men to be

215

sent to the colony. The British Government, thinking that labourers for private hire were needed, was committed to send men who would shortly be free to labour. If men were sent who had long sentences to serve in labouring on public works, it would inflict on the colony the worst of the evils experienced by the older penal colonies. The colonists, however, persisted in wanting their public works done. For the first four years — as the Comptroller General stated in evidence to a Select Committee of the House of Commons in 1856 (Question 1008) — they received convicts of good character. Thereafter, as they clamoured for increased public works, the type of convicts sent became less desirable.

The other qualifications such as health and length of sentence, as enumerated by Willoughby, proved necessary as the years went by. As experience rendered them needful, they were recommended by the Comptroller General and requested by the Governor in despatches to the Colonial Office, which sent the recommendations on to the Home Office, this department in its turn passing them on to the Chairman of Directors of Convict Prisons.

Shortly after the arrival of the first convicts in Western Australia on 1 June 1850, who were to be soon entitled to tickets of leave, Governor Fitzgerald recommended that not more than 300 should follow them because of difficulty in providing accommodation, and of that 300, at least 100 should be long-sentence men, not entitled to tickets of leave before three years. This was because, until the colony recovered a little from its depression, the labour market could not absorb too many ticket-of-leave men discharged on to it, whereas long-sentence men could be employed on the very necessary public works. (P.P., vol. V, Despatch 25/7/1850) Unfortunately Fitzgerald's despatch did not reach the

Colonial Office before 100 men had been sent off by the *Hashemy,* and the Home Office had already contracted for 209 more to be sent. Things were a little congested in the temporary establishment at Fremantle for a while, but hiring-stations for ticket-of-leave men were rapidly established in country towns, so that by May 1853, the Governor was able to ask that 1,000 men be sent annually. In this despatch he made another request, which was to influence the choice of men.

The Governor particularly requested that men of delicate health be not sent out, because they became unemployed and burdensome to the colony. He also remarked that men with diseases of the eye should not be sent, because of the fine white sand at Fremantle and the glare from the sun, both of which were an irritation to the eyes. This was passed on to the Chairman of Directors of Convict Prisons, who replied:

> I will take care that instructions are given that great care be taken by the medical officers in selecting those convicts only for Western Australia who would, on arrival, be fit for work in the colony. (P.P., vol. VII, Labouchere to Kennedy, 4/12/1855)

The question of Irish convicts arose in August 1853. On the 19th of that month, the *Robert Small* arrived from Ireland with 303 prisoners on board, and rapidly following came the *Phoebe Dunbar* on the 30th, with 286 Irish prisoners. These poor creatures — 'many of them enfeebled by disease and incapable of self-control, their imaginations excited by new scenes and their general physical and moral qualities of a low order' — as the Comptroller General reported to the Governor (P.P., vol. VI, 11/9/1854), at once became a problem to the prison authorities. The surgeon's report shows that they came from Mountjoy Prison, Dublin, and were labouring under great mental depression caused by long confinement and the silent system practised in that prison. There were nine deaths on the *Robert Small* and twelve fatal cases of scurvy on the *Phoebe Dunbar*. The surgeon was pleased to notice how the rest of the men responded to a healthy occupation in the open air, and the ample and nutritious diet provided at the Fremantle Establishment; but the Comptroller General found that there had been a remarkable increase in crime in the prison since the arrival of the Irish ships.

> So soon as the permanent prison at Fremantle is complete there will be no objection to receiving a proportion of Irish prisoners, but under no circumstances, I trust, will Irish prisoners be sent to this colony with tickets-of-leave. They should all most decidedly have a term of probationary imprisonment to undergo after landing ...

he continued in his report to the Governor. The sudden arrival of nearly 600 Irish convicts had resulted in their outnumbering the England convicts in the gaol. Governor Fitzgerald was obliged to inform the Secretary of State for the Colonies that much inconvenience had resulted from their arrival, both from their conduct and from the fact that the regulations in force in English and Irish prisons differed as regards length of penal servitude on works, and on the subject of gratuities, allowed in English, but not in Irish, prisons; all of which created discord and discontent among the prisoners. (P.P., vol. VI, Fitzgerald to Newcastle, 30/8/1854, and Enclosure with Despatch of 11/9/1854)

He also apprised the Duke of Newcastle that Irish Roman

Catholics were not likely to be absorbed into labour as easily as English Protestants, both because they were more deficient in capacity and skill, and because most of the settlers preferred taking into their families servants of their own persuasion. 'I wish it to be understood that this feeling is not at all carried to any extent either in bitterness or prejudice,' he ended. He was advised in due course that the Directors of Convict Prisons in Ireland were of the opinion that it would be desirable to stop the despatch of Irish convicts to Western Australia. No more, for the present, would be sent. (P.P., vol. VII, Sir George Grey to Fitzgerald, 8/4/1855) Nevertheless, later ships brought Fenian convicts from both English and Irish gaols to the colony.

The men from the *Robert Small* and the *Phoebe Dunbar* were not the only ones whose conduct gave cause for alarm. The *Stag* and the *Adelaide* from Britain in 1855 had among their convicts men who were 'incorrigibles'; while on 1 January 1858, the ship *Nile* arrived with 268 men of 'the utmost depravity'. So bad had the journey been that it resulted in the strongest representations being made by the Superintendent of Fremantle prison that the arrangements on convict ships should be changed, so as to prevent the men being herded together so much at night in the dark of the holds. He advised that a passage walled with bars should run down the centre of the sleeping apartments so that it would be patrolled with safety by a sentry. The Governor endorsed this recommendation, and added that the water closets should be well and sufficiently lighted at all times, and that the padlocks of doors should not be all of the same pattern, so that if one key should be taken it would open all. (P.P., vol. VIII, Kennedy to Labouchere, Despatch 33, and Enclosure)

With regard to female convicts, Willoughby, and those who

quote him, are entirely correct. Female convicts were never sent to the colony of Western Australia, but it was not for the want of trying. Scarcely two years after the place had become a penal settlement, the Comptroller General reported to the Governor:

> The disproportion of the sexes is one other source of grave consideration. As soon as the necessary accommodation for the male convicts can be provided for, I should suggest for Your Excellency's consideration the erection of an establishment on a limited scale for female convicts.

His Excellency was horrified, and in sending on the recommendation of the Comptroller General to Earl Grey, as he was bound to do, he stated in no uncertain terms:

> I am most decidedly opposed to the measure, as, however desirable under the peculiar circumstances of Western Australia was the introduction of male convicts, that of female convicts I am of opinion was never once wished for. (P.P., vol. VI, Fitzgerald to Grey, 7/6/1852)

This, however, did not end the matter, and for nearly six years the Home Government through different Secretaries of State for the Colonies kept raising the question. The Duke of Newcastle broached the subject to Governor Fitzgerald on 14 December 1853, and 6 March 1854, promising that only female convicts who had undergone a course of preliminary discipline and industrial training should be sent. Fitzgerald replied that public meetings had been held on the question at Perth, York, and Fremantle.

At Perth the majority are decidedly opposed to the measure, equally so at York; at Fremantle the question, I hear, was carried for the introduction of female convicts by a majority consisting principally of ticket-of-leave men, who in my opinion, should never have been permitted a voice in the matter.

He repeated his former assertion that the measure would be one of unmitigated evil for the whole colony, and sent a numerously signed petition from the colonists against such a thing. He also sent the Comptroller General's estimate of the probable expense of constructing a female prison for 200 prisoners — £7,370. (P.P., vol. VI, Fitzgerald to Grey, 3/8/1854, and Enclosure) As the male convict establishment was already proving a heavy drain on the British Treasury, this closed the matter for the best part of two years; but on 16 December 1856 it was suggested by the Directors of Convict Prisons in Ireland that a few female convicts might be sent out. Public meetings were again held; and the colonists and the Governor combined in asking for more free female emigrants to be sent out instead. Finally, in 1858, the Governor received a despatch noting the protests and the resentment provoked by the plan, saying that a new party of female emigrants was about to sail, and dismissing the question of sending out female convicts 'for the present'. It was never to arise again. (P.P., vol. VIII, Labouchere to Kennedy, 17/2/1858)

In 1856, Select Committees of the House of Commons and of the House of Lords were appointed to inquire into the Act relating to Transportation. Evidence was given before the former committee by civil servants and officers of convict prisons, while the Committee of the House of Lords heard evidence from colonists, colonial governors, and officers of convict prisons in the colonies. Both committees heard evidence from Colonel Joshua Jebb, R.E., C.B., Chairman of Directors of Convict Prisons in England.

In the course of evidence, Mr H. Waddington, Under-Secretary of the Home Department, was asked: 'Are you aware whether Western Australia in seeking for convicts has expressed any opinion as to the kind of convicts who ought to go there, or whom it wishes to receive?' His answer was: 'I have not heard any opinion expressed as to that except that they have expressed a very strong desire to have able-bodied men and skilled labourers.'

Mr T.F. Elliott, Assistant Under-Secretary of the Colonial Department, also gave his opinion that it was not worthwhile to go to the expense of sending convicts so great a distance unless they were in good health, and had a certain period of their sentence to serve. (First Report of Select Committee of House of Commons on Transportation, 1856, Questions 206 and 362)

Colonel Jebb, however, giving evidence on transportation, remarked:

> I only look on it as a means of disposing of the men. Under the present agreement and understanding with Western Australia they only want to take the best of the men; it is the worst of the men that we want to get rid of.

He was promptly asked: 'How was that understanding come to?' His reply was: 'By their petitioning. When they first petitioned for convicts to be sent, the understanding was, that they should be the best convicts.' When asked, was the 'understanding' expressed in a letter from the Colonial Office, or in some other form, he floundered: 'I think you will find it in the transportation papers: but without knowing accurately what the terms were, it has been the understanding that the best convicts were to be selected for Western Australia.' (First Report, Questions 1348, 1358, 1359) He gave much the same evidence to the Committee of the House of Lords. Asked what system had been pursued with regard to the selection of convicts for the colony, he replied:

The understanding with Western Australia was that the best of our convicts should be sent there; they consented to receive them upon those terms; and the best and most useful men, artificers and others who were competent to execute works were selected for the first two or three years. After that the selection was necessarily more general. (House of Lords Committee, Question 1142)

It will be noticed that neither of the two Under-Secretaries of the Home and Colonial Departments, who would have been in a position to know of it, referred to any agreement or understanding with the colonists of Western Australia; nor did Earl Grey, who also gave evidence to the Committee of the House of Commons. He had been the Secretary of State for the Colonies at the time of the petition for convicts and he had made the decision to send convicts. He mentioned the fact in evidence that he had promised the colonists convicts of good conduct at the beginning because there was no gaol for them.

Giving evidence to the House of Lords Committee, neither Captain Fitzgerald, Governor at the time that the demand for convicts was made, nor G.F. Moore, former Advocate General of the colony, nor Captain Henderson, Comptroller General in Western Australia, nor R. McBryde Broun, nor T. Yule, two prominent colonists, made any mention of 'agreements' or 'understandings'. It would appear that Colonel Jebb, who was the only person to use those terms, was the one who did all the 'understanding'. He observed Earl Grey's desire that the first convicts should be men of good conduct. He had no direct contact with the colony, as had the Colonial Office through despatches, none of which, printed for Parliament under the title of Convict Discipline and Transportation, bears any reference to an agreement or understanding.

Colonel Jebb pointed out that the selection of men for Western Australia had become more general since the passing of the Act of 1853 which substituted a sentence of penal servitude to be passed at home for all crimes punishable by transportation for less than fourteen years. This meant that there were fewer convicts from which to choose. The Act created anomalies in the administration of justice, for men who received smaller sentences for lesser crimes were kept in prison in England for the whole period, while those who had longer sentences were after several years transported to the colony where they soon gained the relative freedom of tickets of leave. It was amended in 1857 by awarding penal servitude for any crimes punishable by transportation. This meant that the length of sentences corresponded with the old sentences of transportation.

The types of crimes and the sentences they carried before 1853, which meant transportation, can be seen in lists of re-convicted men applying for conditional pardons in Western Australia. The date of their first conviction, crime and sentence are stated on the applications. (CSO 374 and 379, Comptroller General) The crimes include: breaking and entering, arson, cow stealing, assault with intent to rob — 15 years; robbery

224

with violence, receiving stolen goods, house-breaking, cutting and wounding — 14 years; forgery, burglary, manslaughter, felony, larceny, sacrilege, desertion — 10 years; stealing, theft, larceny, demanding money, embezzlement — 7 years.

After 1857, among other crimes with brought transportation were: firing a stack, theft and previous conviction, arson, robbery, receiving stolen goods — 10 years; uttering forged notes — 8 years; larceny, robbery with violence, stealing a watch, shop-breaking, wounding with intent to harm, rape — 7 years; larceny — 6 years. (Return of Ticket-of-leave men recommended for conditional pardons, Package of Odd Despatches, WAA 391)

A Circular of 27 June 1857, addressed to all Judges, Recorders and Chairmen of Quarter Sessions, stated that selection of convicts for Western Australia would be made *as far as possible* from among those whose sentences were for terms of not less than seven years, and they would be removed to the colony after having undergone half their sentence. This worked very well for a time, but in 1859 only 224 convicts arrived in Western Australia, and in 1860 none at all arrived. Consternation began to arise among the colonists, who drew up a memorial regretting the diminished number. This was forwarded to the Colonial Office, which replied that the extreme deficiency of available convicts in England made it difficult to keep up the supply, but added that fresh efforts would be made, a temporary measure being 'to suspend the regulation which requires that all convicts selected for Western Australia shall serve at least half their period of penal servitude in this country before they are eligible'. (P.P., vol. VIII, Fortescue to Kennedy, 1/9/1860) The suspending of this regulation resulted in more convicts arriving, but these were of a much worse character than formerly. At one time in 1861, there were no fewer than from twenty-seven to thirty-seven murderers in Fremantle prison, Governor Kennedy told a Commission inquiring into Transportation and Penal Servitude in 1863 (Report of Commissioners, p. 190), adding:

> I must say that murderers and that class of men are not the most objectionable ... No, the London thief is the worst man we get, and I would rather have any man than him. He will not work if he can help it.

The Report of this Commission on Transportation of 1863 recommended that the seven-year term should be adhered to again, and that some classes of convicts should not be sent to Western Australia. None should be sent who were convicted of unnatural crimes, or who were of unsound mind; and none should be sent who were unfit for manual labour. (Report of Commissioners, p. 52) Its conclusions, reached from the evidence taken, showed that transportation had been a success in the colony and should be continued.

The publication of this Report created a good deal of interest in London. *The Times* reviewed it in the issue of 20 July 1863, and printed a special article on 31 July on the subject of continued transportation. Its issue of 1 August contained a letter by Edward Wilson, proprietor of the Melbourne *Argus*, then in London, which referred to the Commission and 'its most monstrous proposition of sending all your worst convicts, with some slight exceptions, to Western Australia'. His concern, however, was not for that colony; he gave in strong language the point of view of the eastern colonies of Australia. He had been campaigning since 1849 against transportation. Its continuance had been a burning question in the east for some years. Public meetings had been held in Victoria and South Australia, these two colonies contending that they suffered the most, and that Western Australia acted as a funnel to discharge the moral sewage of England into their uncontaminated settlements. Wilson's letter brought a reply on 11 August on behalf of Western Australia by one H.R. Grellet, who promptly brought out a pamphlet: *The Case of England and Western Australia in respect to Transportation* (February 1864), to show that the matter concerned those two countries only. In this year letters appeared in the London *Daily Mail* from the pen of Alexander M'Arthur, a member of the Legislative Council of New South Wales, thundering forth the disgust and indignation of New South Wales that moral ruin should be forced upon it by expiree convicts coming from the west. These letters then appeared as a pamphlet: 'Transportation to Western Australia', privately printed in November 1864 to be distributed in influential quarters.

The latest of these pamphlets to appear was that of Howard Willoughby: *The British Convict in Western Australia: A Visit to the Swan River Settlements*, by the Special Correspondent of the Melbourne *Argus*. In its preface, Willoughby says he was sent by the proprietors of the Melbourne *Argus*, Messrs Wilson and Mackinnon, to gain information about a distant and little-known colony; and he acknowledges the courtesy of the Western Australian Colonial Secretary in placing the Blue Books of the colony at his disposal. It would not appear from the work that he had access to any other official data except these, and the Reports of the Select Committees of the House of Commons and the House of Lords of 1856 and 1863 on Transportation. The phrases he uses are those of the Select Committees. His work originally appeared in the form of letters to the *Argus*; then was brought out as a pamphlet supplement to that journal on 25 June 1864, and later, after 'additions descriptive of the country, its settlements and settlers, and descriptive also of Convict life' had been made, it was published in London in 1865 as a small book of sixty-four pages.

From the foregoing, it will thus be seen that Willoughby, coming to investigate the convict system in Western Australia in 1864, and arriving towards the end of the transportation period, was in effect summing up, not too accurately, the results of various changes in the transportation system, and presenting them as if they had been hard and fast rules, all arranged at the same time, prior to the formation of the penal settlement, in consultation between two parties of equal importance. Several writers visiting Western Australia at this period remark on the capacity of the colonists to delude themselves about the convicts they had themselves asked for; and it would appear that this was the attitude that Willoughby encountered in his researches. (*An Australian Parsonage*, by Mrs Millett, p. 327; *South and Western Australia*, by Anthony Trollope, p. 97) Coming from the *Argus* as Willoughby did (although he states that he was 'unfettered by instructions') and from one of the eastern colonies so opposed to transportation, it was in the interests of Western Australians to present the convict system to him in its best light while they still wished it to continue, which in 1864 most of them still did. It must be recognized, too, that the general public whom Willoughby interviewed would not be aware of the contents of official despatches and memoranda such as are available to the student today and show the reasons and motives for what actually took place. The Home Government did, in fact, try to fulfil the requests — not stipulations — that came from Western Australia from time to time in relation to the convicts; it was the misfortune of the colony, however, to come in at the end of an outdated system subject to changing ideas of social reform, and limited in its general usefulness by the shortness of its duration.

It may be concluded that in the first three years of penal settlement the convicts sent out had been selected for good conduct, and that after that, the colony had had to take what it could get. The colonists had no say in the matter, and there is no evidence to show that they cared. What they wanted was the convicts as a work force, and the overseas capital which the establishment of the penal settlement would bring to inject new life into the colony's finances. As for the effects of the convicts on the moral tone of the community — the community was so scattered, and the convicts so dispersed in the vast country-side that they really made little impression, with their relatively small numbers, on the established order to which they had come. If they were not all, and always, 'good' convicts, nevertheless they and the system which supported them, in the eighteen years between the arrival of the first and the last convict ship, had the effect of setting the tottering colony firmly on its feet.

# *Appendix C*

*Some Figures Showing the Type and Prevalence of Offences
Committed During the Convict Period*

THE Papers printed for Parliament on Convict Discipline and
Transportation shed some interesting light on the behaviour
of convicts after they had gained their tickets of leave, and a
certain amount of freedom. For the years 1854 to 1858,
abstracts were made showing the offences and convictions of
both free and ticket-of-leave men at different centres all over
the colony. As the number of prisoners grew larger, this
method of tabulating was changed. The returns of free men
convicted were not included, and comparison of free and
convict crime becomes more difficult. (It should be
remembered that some of the 'free' men, though not a large
number at this early date, would be expirees.) Later years
show only Returns of offences for which ticket-of-leave men
were convicted, and in some years even these were not kept.
For this reason, the Return for 1865 cannot be given.

Table 1 has been simplified by leaving out the numbers of
men at the different centres for each crime, and taking only
the total number in the colony for each crime. Table 2 is given
exactly as it appeared.

A glance at the population figures for 1855 shows that the
total population was then 11,976. This included military,

230

prisoners in gaol, conditional pardon and ticket-of-leave holders, as well as 3,538 females (of whom 1,294 were under twelve years of age); and 4,073 free males (of whom 1,148 were under twelve years of age). (*Western Australian Almanack for 1856*, p. 68) In 1866, the total population was 21,065, of whom 13,584 were males. (Blue Book for 1866, p. 132)

## Table 1

*Abstract of Offences and Convictions in the Colony of Free and Ticket-of-Leave Men, comparatively for the half year ending 30 June 1855*[1]

| Nature of Offence | Free Convicted | Ticket-of-Leave Convicted |
|---|---|---|
| Absconding | 6 | 27 |
| Assault (common) | 54 | 26 |
| Burglary | 3 | 4 |
| Drunkenness | 172 | 189 |
| Felony | 3 | 3 |
| Forgery and uttering | 0 | 3 |
| Illegally at large being armed | 0 | 3 |
| Larceny | 6 | 12 |
| Misdemeanour | 89 | 56 |
| Manslaughter | 1 | 0 |
| Murder | 1 | 1 |
| Perjury | 0 | 2 |
| Rape | 1 | 0 |
| Robbery | 11 | 20 |
| Sheep-stealing | 2 | 1 |
| Stealing in dwelling | 5 | 16 |
| Not particularized | 113 | 129 |
| | 467 | 492 |

---

[1] Parliamentary Papers on Convict Discipline and Transportation, volume VII, p. 165.

## Table 2

*Return of Offences for which Ticket-of-Leave Holders have been convicted by Magistrates during the year 1866*[2]

| | |
|---|---|
| Absconding | 47 |
| Assaults (common) | 35 |
| Burglary | 12 |
| Drunkenness | 429 |
| Felony | 20 |
| Forgery | 5 |
| Larceny | 72 |
| Rape | 1 |
| Unnatural crime | 1 |
| Wounding with intent | 3 |
| Miscellaneous | 592 |
| | 1,217 |

[2] Annual Reports on Convict Establishments, p. 12.

# Notes

## CHAPTER 1

1   The date is derived from Sykes's age given in the Census of March 1851, H.O.107/2344, bk 1, p. 297. The place is stated in one of the letters.

2   William Sykes, senior, is not mentioned in the Census of 1841; his trade is given on his son's marriage registration at Somerset House. In the Census of 1851, Mrs Thirza Sykes has become Thirza Gascoigne, widow, and her son William Sykes, unmarried, twenty-four, is living with her. Reference as above.

3   Census of 1851, H.O.107/2344, bk 1, p. 1, and H.O.107/2345, bk 4.

4   Marriage Certificate 262804, Somerset House.

5   The movement had started in Glasgow, and the London Mechanics' Institute was opened in 1826. By 1841 there were 610 institutes throughout England. (E.L. Woodward, *The Age of Reform*, p. 475.)

6   J.L. and B. Hammond, *The Village Labourer*, p. 187.

7   G.M. Young (ed.), *Early Victorian England*, vol. 1, pp. 50–51. A puddler was a man who raked and stirred molten iron in rows of small furnaces until it was ready for the hammer. He was a key man in the iron industry and would take on assistants or 'underhands' to whom he would pay a wage. The puddler himself was paid by the work done. He might make from 5s. to 6s. a day. He was usually a picked man, of powerful physique, capable of working in the heat and glare of furnaces. It is not known whether William Sykes was head puddler or underhand. He is described in the arraignment at his trial as 'forgeman', and in the prison register as 'puddler'.

8   As described by the reporter of the *Sheffield and Rotherham*

234

*Independent,* this was 'a weapon of a peculiar construction, a piece of wood about 20 inches long, with a heavy wooden ball depending from a flexible thong at the end. The ... flail ... could be attached to the wrist by a leathern loop.'

9   This account of the events of the night of 10 October 1865 is compiled from the evidence of various witnesses given on oath at the Leeds Assizes of December 1865, and printed in full in the *Sheffield and Rotherham Independent* each day from 22 to 26 December 1865.

10  *Sheffield and Rotherham Independent,* 13/10/1865.

11  ibid., 26/10/1865.

12  ibid., 22/12/1865.

13  ibid., 26/12/1865.


CHAPTER 2


1   *Cornhill Magazine,* vol. XIII, p. 497.

2   Some of this sermonizing is obviously that of Hargreaves himself, and shows the man — a good man, but of the lower classes, who can quote Scripture at great length, but does not know when he has gone on too long and reached an effect of bathos. It may occur to the reader, however, from the sudden difference of style of the middle portion of the letter, that Hargreaves lifted this part from some discourse or tract, the better to admonish William Sykes.

3   CSO 606, p. 53, and *Perth Gazette,* 19/7/1867.

4   ibid.

5   The smallest ship from Britain was the *Mermaid,* 472 tons. There were smaller ones from Calcutta bringing only a few prisoners; and one large one, the *Caduceus,* a Government transport, 1,106 tons, which brought one prisoner only, and forty-seven syces, from Bombay. It was fitted for horses, and returned to Bombay with 150 horses, delivered at Fremantle at a price of £40 a head, from the property of Samuel Phillips of Toodyay. They were for the use of the British army in India at the time of the Mutiny.

6   C.O.18/55 and 46, folio 185.

7 Colin A. Browning, *England's Exiles*, pp. 2–3.

8 Register R 15, Fremantle prison.

9 J.T. Reilly, *Reminiscences of Fifty Years' Residence in Western Australia*, p. 3.

10 John Boyle O'Reilly, *Moondyne*.

11 *Cornhill Magazine*, vol. XIII, p. 501.

12 ibid., p. 500.

13 Colin A. Browning, op. cit., p. 97.

CHAPTER 3

1 C.O.18/39, Hutt to Stanley, 15/8/1845.

2 *Fremantle Observer*, 23/5/1831 (HS703). This is a photostat of the newspaper; the whereabouts of the original is unknown. In *The Colonization of Australia*, Professor Mills quotes (pp. 71–72, footnote) the passage on the demand for convicts, but gives it an ending which is not in the photostat. He remarks, however, that he could not obtain a copy of the *Fremantle Observer*, but quoted it as it was reported in *The Times* of 23/11/1831.

3 C.O.18/50, Fitzgerald to Grey, 3/3/1849.

4 ibid.

5 ibid.

6 *The Inquirer*, 14/8/1850 and 19/6/1850.

7 P.P., vol. V, Fitzgerald to Grey, 25/7/1850, Enclosure of Comptroller General.

8 *Perth Gazette*, 28/6/1850.

9 P.P., vol. V, Fitzgerald to Grey, Enclosure.

10 *The Inquirer*, 10/7/1850.

11 CSO 201, Comptroller General to Colonial Secretary, 6/7/1850.

12 *The Inquirer*, 17/7/1850.

13 P.P., vol. V, Fitzgerald to Grey, 25/7/1850, Enclosure.

14 P.P., vol. VIII, Kennedy to Newcastle, 24/8/1860, Buildings erected between the years 1854 and 1859 inclusive.

15 The figures given are of those who actually arrived. The shipping lists in CSO volumes give the numbers despatched from England, and these are quoted in Kimberly's *History of West Australia*. An Appendix in Gertzel's 'The Convict System in Western Australia, 1850–1870' gives the number of deaths on each ship, and the number of those who actually entered the gaol. The latter figures are quoted on p. 40. The number of deaths was never more than from one to three per ship, with the exception of two, which had nine and ten deaths, so there is not a great deal of variation in the numbers.

16 Report of Select Committee of the House of Lords on Transportation, 1856, Captain Henderson, Question 1008.

17 P.P., vol. VI, Fitzgerald to Newcastle, 13/8/1853.

18 P.P., vol. VII, Report of Works, July–December 1854.

19 ibid., January–June 1855.

20 ibid., July–December 1855.

21 P.P., vol. VII, Sub-enclosure of the Clerk of Works, with Despatch of 28/7/1856, also Enclosure, 2, Minute of the Convict Finance Board.

22 CSO 379, Acting Comptroller General to Colonial Secretary, 9/12/1857.

23 ibid.

24 P.P., vol. VIII, Enclosure of Comptroller General for the year ending 31/12/1859.

25 *Historical Records of Australia*, Series I, vol. XIX, pp. 332–35.

26 P.P., vol. V, Fitzgerald to Grey, 7/11/1850.

27 P.P., vol. VIII, Kennedy to Lytton, 15/4/1859, and Newcastle to Kennedy, 13/8/1859.

28 Report of Select Committee of the House of Lords on Transportation, 1856, Question 178.

29 *The Cape Times*, 1/8/1935, Article 'A Civil Engineer of 1820', by Professor Snape, Civil Engineering Department, University of Cape Town. Census of 1851, H.O.107/1855, bk 2a.

30 *Perth Gazette*, 1/7/1848.

31 ibid., 11/1/1840.

32  C.O.18/40, 28/7/1845 and 15/8/1845.

33  C.O.18/41, 30/10/1845.

34  C.O.18/56, 28/5/1850.

35  Minutes of the Executive Council, 25/2/1849 and 19/10/1849.

36  *The Inquirer*, 16/4/1851.

37  Notebook of John Williams, 1842.

38  *The Inquirer*, 14/11/1855 and 22/10/1856.

39  *The West Australian*, 16/2/1888, Article on Governor Fitzgerald by an unnamed old colonist who had known him.

40  *The Inquirer*, 10/7/1850.

41  Diary of Alfred Stone, *W.A.H.S. Journal*, vol. 1, 6, p. 31.

42  Reminiscences of James Kennedy (in possession of Mr Hasluck).

43  C.O.18/55, Fitzgerald to Grey, 25/11/1850.

44  Mrs Millett, *An Australian Parsonage*, p. 19; *The Inquirer*, 20/5/1857, and Hale Diary, 21/9/1861.

45  CSF 38, Colonial Secretary to Commandant, 15/6/1854.

46  J.K. Ewers, *The Perth Boys' School*, pp. 74–75.

47  *The Inquirer*, 4/9/1850.

48  ibid., 24/1/1855.

49  CSO 398, Comptroller General to Colonial Secretary, 15/3/1858.

50  *Perth Gazette*, 9/4/1858.

51  ibid., 28/5/1858.

52  CSR 809, 22/7/1875.

53  Blue Book, 1870–71, p. 68.

54  CSO 337, 9/1/1855.

55  *Possum*, 14/1/1888, Western Australian Gallery of Celebrities.

56  ibid., 21/1/1888.

57  Buildings ascribed to Richard Jewell are: the Perth gaol, the Old Railway Station, the Boys' and Girls' School at James Street, the Pensioners' Barracks, the Town Hall, Wesley Church, Independent Church (Trinity), Public Offices, the Deanery, the New Convent, the Masonic Hall and many other buildings in other parts of the colony. He retired from the position of Director of Public Works in 1884.

James Manning had charge of the whole of the prison buildings at Fremantle, Government House, Perth, and in conjunction with Richard Jewell, the Town Hall and the Pensioners' Barracks. He constructed numerous bridges throughout the colony, including the wooden Fremantle traffic bridge. He retired from the Convict Department in 1872.

58  *Western Australian Almanack* for 1860, also COD, Odd Despatches, WAA391.

59  CSF 42, 22/5/1860, and A523, Clerk of Works Letter Book, 19/4/1860.

60  *The Inquirer*, 11/3/1859 and 18/3/1859.

61  ibid., 19/12/1866.

62  *Government Gazette*, 27/7/1858.

63  *The Inquirer*, 25/4/1866.

64  ibid., 9/1/1867.

65  CSO 606, p. 53 and CSO 626, p. 104.


CHAPTER 4


1  P.P., vol. VIII, Memo of buildings created between 1854–59, Enclosure with Despatch of Kennedy to Newcastle, 24/8/1860.

2  P.P., vol. VI, p. 244.

3  P.P., vol. VI, Fitzgerald to Grey, 25/5/1853, Surgeon's Report.

4  A set of these duck suits may still be seen at Fremantle prison, and a set of the parti-coloured clothes which were worn by runaway prisoners on their recapture. These are made of a stout felt-like material. The front of the coat and waistcoat is black, and the back, mustard yellow, stamped not very liberally with broad arrows. The sleeves of the coat are parti-coloured, and though there are no trousers to this set, they were parti-coloured too. The gaol steward's report for 19/1/1858 mentions that '22 parti-coloured suits for Runaways' had been made (P.P., vol. VIII, p. 90). Sets of irons ranging in weight from fourteen to twenty-eight pounds still remain at the prison, together with cat-o'-nine-tails, some with cord and some with leather 'tails', and the tripod of dark oiled wood to which prisoners were tied to be flogged. Also to be seen is a kind of

corset of leather, said to be for the protection of the kidneys during flogging.

5   Letter Book and Memo Book of Comptroller General, C3, Fremantle prison.

6   P.P., vol. VII, Kennedy to Russell, 5/9/1855, Enclosure.

7   Annual Reports, Bruce to Granville, 26/2/1869.

8   Register R 15, Fremantle prison.

9   List of Convict Ships arrived in the Colony, WAA128.

10   P.P., vol. VII, Fitzgerald to Sir George Grey, 18/6/1855, Enclosure of Board of Medical Officers.

11   This was the second voyage of the *Pyrenees*. Several of the convict transports made two voyages, including the *Norwood*, which had come out in 1862 as well as in 1867.

12   List of Convict Ships arrived in the Colony, WAA128.

13   *Government Gazette*, 13/3/1855.

14   Visited by the writer, 7/12/1957. The Moondyne Springs are in a wild and lonely locality still well off the beaten track. They rise in several places on the granite-strewn sides of a gully running down to the Avon River in the general neighbourhood of Toodyay. Nearby is a cave, or rather a formation of three large granite boulders making a lean-to shelter, said to have been used by Johns. Because he frequented this place, its name was pinned on to him.

15   C.W. Ferguson, 'Moondyne Joe', in *Sunday Times*, 27/5/1928.

16   *The Inquirer*, 5/9/1866.

17   Account of Henry Passmore, a former gaoler, *Western Mail*, 1906, requoted *Western Mail*, 29/10/1953.

18   *The Inquirer*, 13/3/1867.

19   C.W. Ferguson, op. cit.

20   *The Inquirer*, 7/11/1860 and 28/11/1860. Measles had first appeared in Western Australia in severe epidemic form in November 1860. Most of the Government officers and the whole town, both old and young, had been laid low with them, so they were still a sufficiently topical subject for such an allusion.

21   C.W. Ferguson, op. cit.

22   *The Inquirer*, 21/11/1866 and 28/11/1866.

23 This bridge, begun in December 1864, put into use in November 1866, and its approaches and rails finished in the following year, was built entirely by convict labour, from the designs of Captain Grain, R.E., who had succeeded Captain Wray, and Mr Manning, Clerk of Works. It replaced a ferry which had until then been the only way of crossing the river at Fremantle in order to proceed to Perth. Made of stout jarrah timber, and built high in the middle for boats to pass underneath, the bridge rapidly got the name of 'The Bridge of Styx', or 'Hampton's Folly'. Nevertheless, it was essential to the communications of the capital and the port, and it lasted well into the twentieth century.

24 *South Western News*, 8/4/1932.

25 P.P., vol. VIII, Kennedy to Newcastle, 24/8/1860, Enclosure.

26 *The Inquirer*, 21/1/1842. Chronological Register of Events in Western Australia for 1841.

27 Australind was the name given to an area on the coast near Bunbury. A settlement scheme promoted by a London body called the Western Australian Company was put into operation there in 1841, after much bungling and changing of plans produced by rumours and slow methods of communication with the colony. In 1843, the affairs of the company were wound up, and most of the settlers who had come out to Australind drifted away to other parts of the colony or left it altogether.

28 *Government Gazette*, 13/3/1846.

29 *The Inquirer*, 22/4/1846.

30 *Western Australian Almanack*, May 1862. Mrs Millett, *An Australian Parsonage*, p. 163. (The writer has often travelled on the Wanneroo road while it still had its wooden 'cheese' foundation.)

31 *The Inquirer*, 28/8/1867.

32 ibid., 4/9/1867 and 2/10/1867.

33 Annual Reports, Hampton to Chandos, 21/3/1868.

34 CSF 42, 3/2/1859.

35 C. Gertzel, 'The Convict System in Western Australia, 1850-1870', pp. 37–39, 46.

36 *The Inquirer*, 25/11/1868.

37 ibid., 19/2/1868.

38  J.T. Reilly, *Reminiscences of Fifty Years' Residence in Western Australia,* pp. 145–48.

39  ibid., pp. 143–45, W.H. Kimberly, *History of West Australia,* pp. 244–45.

40  COD, Odd Despatches 1871-99, WAA391.

41  W.H. Kimberly, op. cit., p. 244.

42  Register R15, Fremantle prison, 26/11/1867.

43  Annual Reports, Return of Works for 1868.

CHAPTER 6

1   CSO 708, Memo of Comptroller General to Governor, 2/2/1872.

2   ibid., 13/2/1872 and 16/2/1872.

3   CSO 708, Resident Magistrate of Vasse to Colonial Secretary, 13/2/1872.

4   Governors' Despatches, vol. XII, Weld to Carnarvon, 9/9/1874.

5   ibid., vol. XI, Weld to Kimberley, 22/2/1872.

6   ibid., vol. XII, no. 97, 11/8/1875.

7   Blue Book, 1875–76, Return of Probation and Re-Convicted men on Public Works.

8   Toodyay Resident Magistrate's Letter Book, 1867–83, 24/6/1878.

9   This name appears on maps as late as 1889. It is thought that 'King Dick' was an Aborigine. There was a huge jarrah tree at one point on the road called 'King Dick's Tree' which lasted to within living memory. Distinctive trees such as this are known in other districts and appear to have been landmarks for Aborigines.

10  P.P., vol. VII, p. 148, Report of Works from Guildford.

11  Diary of Henry de Burgh.

12  G.F. Moore, *Diary of Ten Years of an Early Settler in Western Australia,* p. 68.

13  Map 11A, West Toodyay. Lands Department, Perth.

14  P.P., vol. V, Fitzgerald to Grey, 16/8/1851.

15  Surveyor-General's Letter Book, 1850–62, 13/6/1853.

16  P.P., vol. VI, Fitzgerald to Newcastle, 20/12/1853.

17  Map 12C, Toodyay, Glebe and Pensioners' Lots. Lands Department.

18  J.R. Wollaston, *Albany Journals, 1848–1856*, p. 149.

19  Maps 12 and 12B, Toodyay (Newcastle). Lands Department.

20  *Government Gazette*, 6/5/1910, p. 1034.

21  *Early Days*, vol. VI, p. 9.

22  J.R. Wollaston, op. cit., p. 169.

23  Interview with Mrs E. Bostock, daughter of S.P. Phillips, 14/6/1955.

24  J.J. Roche, *John Boyle O'Reilly: His Life, Poems and Speeches*, p. 647, 'Western Australia'.

25  John Forrest, *Explorations in Australia*, pp. 19–20.

26  *The Inquirer*, 8/9/1869.

27  ibid., 6/10/1869.

28  Interview with Mrs Bostock, 14/6/1955.

29  Ernest Giles, *Australia Twice Traversed*, vol. II., p. 242.

30  *The Inquirer*, 17/11/1875.

31  ibid., 24/11/1875.

32  CSO 708, Resident Magistrate, Newcastle, to Colonial Secretary, 27/2/1872.

33  Annual Reports, Report of Clerk of Works, 18/2/1864 and 11/2/1865.

34  Resident Magistrate's Letter Book, 18/5/1878 and 5/7/1881.

35  Blue Book, 1875–76, Convict Population.

36  Resident Magistrate's Letter Book, 30/7/1880.

37  Register R 15, Fremantle prison.

38  Burial Register, Church of St Mary, Greasbrough, England. As there was no registration of the death of Myra Sykes recorded at Somerset House, London, it occurred to the writer that she might have married again and changed her surname. The Marriage Register of St Mary's revealed that she had indeed done so. After the death of William Sykes, she married Charles Mitchell of Greasbrough on 19 November 1892. The Burial Register showed that she died two years later and was buried as Myra Mitchell on 20 December 1894.

39  Register R 15, Fremantle prison.

40  Annual Reports, Hampton to Cardwell, 18/2/1866.

41  J.R. Wollaston, op. cit., p. 228.

42  *The Inquirer*, 17/7/1855. Reports of meetings held on the subject of female convicts. Also, M.B. Hale, *The Transportation Question*, pp. 45–63.

43  P.P., vol. VII, Abstract of Offences and Convictions in the Colony of Free and Ticket-of-Leave Men, comparatively for the half year ending 30/6/1855, p. 165. Also, Annual Reports on the Convict Establishment, p. 12.

44  Minutes of the Executive Council, 4/5/1857.

45  P.P., vol. VII, Labouchere to Kennedy, 25/1/1856.

46  ibid.

47  CSF 42, 7/3/1860.

48  *The Inquirer*, 27/7/1870. Census Returns.

49  J.T. Reilly, *Reminiscences of Fifty Years' Residence in Western Australia*, p. 49.

50  C. Gibson, *Life Among Convicts*, vol. II, p. 268.

51  *Perth Gazette*, 28/6/1872.

52  W.H. Knight, *Western Australia: Its History, Progress, Condition and Prospects*, p. 119.

53  Journal of Thomas Scott (HS 494).

54  *The Inquirer*, 19/10/1870.

55  C. Gertzel, 'The Convict System in Western Australia, 1850–1870', pp. 121–25.

56  Resident Magistrate's Letter Book, 31/12/1890.

57  Registrar-General, Births, Deaths and Marriages, Perth, 48/1891.

58  Resident Magistrate's Letter Book, 1/3/1891.

59  ibid., 2/10/1891.

60  CSO 708, Resident Magistrate to Colonial Secretary, 27/2/1872.

61  Public Works Department 4681, No. 1819, Plan of Police Quarters and Female Cells, undated; No. 4713, Plan of Police Quarters, contract completed 26/6/1920.

62  In the packet of Sykes Letters at the Archives, there is one more

letter to which no allusion has been made. It is an application to be made a constable, addressed from the Toodyay hospital, and is unsigned. The data contained in it do not fit with the facts and dates of Sykes's record in the Register at Fremantle prison; and it was not in the bundle as first copied. It is possible it was among the papers blowing about at the time of the demolition, but was handed in much later, and added to the Sykes Letters because it came from the same place. Before this research was done, for all anyone knew, it might have been his application.

63   J.S. Battye, *Western Australia: A History from its Discovery to the Inauguration of the Commonwealth*, Appendix IV, Statistical Summary.

64   Gilbert Parker, *Round the Compass in Australia*, p. 387.

65   This information was given by the official grave-digger at Toodyay, Ted Chapman, who said that beyond the last line of graves, numbered 307–323 on the plan of the cemetery, there are three rows of other graves. This coincides with older accounts of the paupers' and convicts' unhallowed burial ground at Old Toodyay. The graves in the present Toodyay cemetery date from the seventies onward, and have been searched vainly for the name of William Sykes. There is no undertaker in Toodyay, and the Road Board has only a torn and undocumented plan of the cemetery.

# Bibliography

## ABBREVIATIONS

| | |
|---|---|
| H.O. | Home Office. |
| C.O. | Colonial Office. |
| CSO | Colonial Secretary's Office (Perth). |
| CSR | Incoming Correspondence of the Colonial Secretary's Office. |
| CSF | Outgoing Correspondence of the Colonial Secretary's Office. |
| COD | Colonial Office Despatches. |
| P.P. | Parliamentary Papers on Convict Discipline and Transportation, 1849–65. (In The Western Australian Archives, these are bound in volumes numbered IV–VIII. References are therefore given as P.P., volume number, and date of particular despatch.) |
| WAA | Western Australian Archives |
| HS | Historical Society |
| Annual Reports | Annual Reports on the Convict Establishment, 1865–69. |

## OFFICIAL DOCUMENTS

*In the Public Record Office, Chancery Lane, London*

Home Office, Census of 1841, (H.O.107/1329) district of Wath, Rotherham, Yorkshire.

Home Office, Census of 1851, (H.O.107/2344) district of Kimberworth, Rotherham. (H.O.107/2345) district of Wath, Rotherham.

*In Somerset House, London*
Registers of Births, Deaths and Marriages.

*In the Comptroller General's Department, formerly housed at Fremantle prison*
Convict Register, R 15.
Letter and Memo Book of Comptroller General, C 3.

*In the Premier's Department, Perth*
Minutes of the Executive Council.

*At the Registrar-General's Office, Perth*
Register of Deaths, 48/1891.

*In the State Archives, Battye Library, Perth*
Annual Reports on the Convict Establishment, 1865–69.
Blue Books, 1850–90.
Clerk of Works Letter Book.
Colonial Office Despatches, Odd Despatches 1871–99.
Colonial Secretary's Office Records, Incoming and Outgoing
    Correspondence.

*Government Gazettes*
Governors' Despatches.
List of Convict Ships arrived in the Colony.
Microfilm of Public Record Office, Colonial Office Documents.
Parliamentary Papers on Convict Discipline and Transportation,
    1849–65.
Report of Commissioners appointed to inquire into the operation of Acts
    relating to Transportation and Penal Servitude, 1863.
Resident Magistrate's Letter Books, Newcastle, 1867–83, and 1884–97.
Rules and Regulations for the Convict Department, Western Australia, 1862.
Select Committee of the House of Commons on Transportation, 1856.
Select Committee of the House of Lords on Transportation, 1856.
Surveyor-General's Letter Book, 1850–62.

## NEWSPAPERS

*The Cape Times*, 1935.

*Fremantle Observer*, 1831.

*Illustrated London News*, 1849–50.

*The Inquirer*, 1840–80.

*Perth Gazette*, 1833–78.

*Possum*, 1888.

*Sheffield and Rotherham Independent*, 1865.

*The Sheffield Daily Telegraph*, 28/10/1865.

*South Western News*, 8/4/1932.

*Sunday Times*, 1928.

*Swan River News and Western Australian Chronicle*, 1844–47.

*The Times*, 1831.

*Toodyay Herald*, 1913–31.

*The West Australian*, 1888.

*Western Australian Almanacks*, 1849–89.

*Western Mail*, 1953.


## JOURNALS

*Cornhill Magazine*, January–June, 1866.

*Early Days*, a publication of the Western Australian Historical Society.

*Journals of the Western Australian Historical Society*, volumes I, II and IV.


## MANUSCRIPTS

The Convict System in Western Australia, 1850–1870, by Cherry Gertzel. WAA, PR/349.

Diaries of Bishop Hale. WAA309.

Diary of Henry de Burgh. WAA248.

Diary of Sophia Phillips. HS 458.

Journal of Lockier Burges, April to September 1841, and April 1845 to July 1846. HS 470.

Journal of Samuel Burges, November 1840 to March 1841. HS 165.

Journal of Thomas Scott, 1870–1874. HS 494.

Notebook of John Williams, 1842. WAA678.

Reminiscences of James Kennedy (in the possession of Mr P. Hasluck).

The Sykes Letters, copies (in the possession of Mr P. Hasluck).

The Sykes Letters, originals. WAA564A.

PRINTED WORKS

Backhouse, James, *A Narrative of a Visit to the Australian Colonies*, London, 1847.

Battye, J.S., *Western Australia: A History from its Discovery to the Inauguration of the Commonwealth*, London, 1924.

Browning, Colin Arrott, *England's Exiles*, London, 1842.

Du Cane, Colonel Sir Edmund, *The Punishment and Prevention of Crime*, London, 1885.

Ewers, J.K., *The Perth Boys' School*, Perth, 1947.

Favenc, Ernest, *The Explorers of Australia*, Christchurch, 1908.

Forrest, John, *Explorations in Australia*, London, 1875.

Gibson, Charles B., *Life Among the Convicts*, 2 vols, London, 1863.

Giles, Ernest, *Australia Twice Traversed*, 2 vols, London, 1889.

Grellet, H.R., *The Case of England and Western Australia in respect to Transportation*, London, 1864.

Grey, Earl, *The Colonial Policy of Lord John Russell's Administration*, 2 vols, London, 1853.

Hale, Mathew B., *The Transportation Question*, Cambridge, 1857.

Hammond, J.L. and Barbara, *The Village Labourer*, 2 vols, Guild Books, 1948.

—— *The Bleak Age*, Pelican Books, 1947.

Herman, Morton, *Early Australian Architects and Their Work*, Sydney, 1954.

Hitchcock, J.K., *The History of Fremantle*, Fremantle, 1929.

Kimberly, W.B., *History of West Australia*, Melbourne, 1897.

Knight, W.H., *Western Australia: Its History, Progress, Condition and Prospects*, Perth, 1870.

M'Arthur, Alexander, *Transportation to Western Australia*, London, 1864.

Millett, Mrs Edward, *An Australian Parsonage*, London, 1872.

Mills, R.C., *The Colonization of Australia (1829–1842)*, London, 1915.

Moore, George F., *Diary of Ten Years of an Early Settler in Western Australia*, London, 1884.

Nicolay, the Reverend C.G., *The Handbook of Western Australia, 1881–96*, Perth, 1896.

O'Brien, Eris, *The Foundation of Australia*, London, 1937.

O'Reilly, John Boyle, *Moondyne*, Melbourne, 1880.

Oman, C.W., *England in the Nineteenth Century*, London, 1913.

Parker, Gilbert, *Round the Compass in Australia*, London, 1892.

Reilly J.T., *Reminiscences of Fifty Years' Residence in Western Australia*, Perth, 1903.

Roche, James Jeffrey, *John Boyle O'Reilly: His Life, Poems and Speeches*, New York, 1891.

Thomas, Alf. T., *A History of Toodyay*, Perth, 1949.

Trollope, Anthony, *South and Western Australia*, London, 1875.

Willoughby, H., *The British Convict in Western Australia*, London, 1865.

Wollaston, the Reverend J.R., *Albany Journals, 1848–1856*, Perth, 1954.

Woodward, E.L., *The Age of Reform*, London, 1938.

Young, G.M. (ed.), *Early Victorian England*, 2 vols, London, 1934.

# Index